Moving to Malaysia

A guide for prospective expatriates

By Dr Alex Bugeja, PhD

Created in part using the Qyx AI Book Creator

See "About this book" in the Introduction

Introduction

Chapter 1 Why Malaysia?

Chapter 2 Visas and Immigration

Chapter 3 Finding a Place to Live

Chapter 4 The Cost of Living in Malaysia

Chapter 5 Healthcare in Malaysia

Chapter 6 Education: Options for Expat Families

Chapter 7 Working in Malaysia: Job Market and Business Opportunities

Chapter 8 Setting Up Your Finances: Banking and Taxes

Chapter 9 Transportation: Getting Around Malaysia

Chapter 10 Language: Communicating in a Multilingual Society

Chapter 11 Malaysian Culture: Customs and Etiquette

Chapter 12 Religion and Religious Harmony in Malaysia

Chapter 13 Food: A Culinary Journey Through Malaysia's Diverse Flavors

Chapter 14 Shopping and Entertainment in Malaysia

Chapter 15 Travel and Tourism: Exploring Malaysia's Beauty

Chapter 16 Nature and Wildlife: Experiencing Malaysia's Biodiversity

Chapter 17 Safety and Security in Malaysia

Chapter 18 Social Life and Making Friends in Malaysia

Chapter 19 Housing: Renting and Buying Property

Chapter 20 Utilities and Communication Services

Chapter 21 Domestic Help and Daily Life Essentials

Chapter 22 Legal Matters: Understanding the Malaysian Legal System

Chapter 23 Retirement in Malaysia: A Peaceful and Affordable Option

Chapter 24 Investing in Malaysia: Opportunities and Considerations

Chapter 25 Adapting to Life in Malaysia: Tips for a Smooth Transition

Introduction

Moving to a new country is a life-changing experience, filled with a mix of excitement and trepidation. Choosing Malaysia as your new home opens doors to a vibrant and diverse world, steeped in rich history, breathtaking landscapes, and a welcoming multicultural society. Whether you are seeking new career opportunities, a more relaxed lifestyle, or a chance to immerse yourself in a melting pot of cultures, Malaysia has something to offer everyone.

This book is designed as your comprehensive guide to navigating the exciting journey of moving to Malaysia. It is aimed specifically at prospective expatriates, offering practical advice and insights to make your transition as seamless as possible. From understanding the visa requirements and finding a place to live, to exploring the cost of living, healthcare, education, and work opportunities, we'll delve into the essential aspects of expat life in Malaysia.

Beyond the practicalities, this book also aims to unveil the heart and soul of Malaysia. You'll gain an appreciation for the cultural nuances, the delicious cuisine, the abundance of travel destinations, and the unique blend of tradition and modernity that makes Malaysia so captivating. We'll touch on aspects of daily life, from transportation and communication to social etiquette and safety, providing you with the knowledge and confidence to thrive in your new environment.

Whether you are a seasoned expat or embarking on your first international move, this guide will equip you with the necessary tools to make informed decisions and to embrace the enriching experience of living in Malaysia. Welcome to a world of possibilities!

About this book

The author, Dr Alex Bugeja, is the Founder & CEO of Traffikoo, a Texas company specializing in online advertising, AI tools, and

SaaS solutions. He is originally from Malta and now lives in Texas.

This book was created in part using the Qyx AI Book Creator, a project developed and maintained by Traffikoo. Qyx AI Book Creator is a powerful and affordable AI ghostwriter, capable of creating entire books on virtually any subject. It is suitable for making books to sell to others, as well as for personal use. Its books are perfectly useable as is - or as drafts for those wishing to edit them and add their own personal touches.

Besides serving as a guide to moving to Malaysia, we hope this book also inspires you to try out Qyx AI Book Creator for yourself.

CHAPTER ONE: Why Malaysia?

Malaysia, a Southeast Asian gem, has emerged as a popular destination for expatriates from all corners of the globe. But what makes this tropical nation such a magnet for those seeking a new life abroad? The answer lies in a captivating blend of factors that create an appealing lifestyle, offering something for almost everyone.

A Strategic Location in the Heart of Southeast Asia

Malaysia occupies a strategic position in Southeast Asia, bridging the continents of Asia and Oceania. This makes it an ideal hub for both business and leisure travel. With excellent air and sea connectivity, you'll find it easy to explore neighboring countries such as Thailand, Singapore, Indonesia, Vietnam, and the Philippines.

A Melting Pot of Cultures and Ethnicities

Malaysia boasts a rich tapestry of cultures, with a harmonious blend of Malay, Chinese, Indian, and indigenous influences. This cultural diversity permeates every aspect of life, from the colorful festivals and traditions to the delectable cuisine and warm hospitality. As an expat, you'll have the opportunity to immerse yourself in a truly multicultural environment, broadening your horizons and embracing new perspectives.

A Relatively Low Cost of Living

Compared to many Western countries and even some other Asian nations, Malaysia offers a relatively low cost of living. Housing, food, transportation, and entertainment are generally affordable, allowing you to stretch your budget further and enjoy a comfortable lifestyle. This affordability is particularly attractive to retirees and those seeking a more financially sustainable way of life.

Modern Infrastructure and Amenities

Malaysia boasts modern infrastructure and amenities, making daily life convenient and comfortable. From world-class shopping malls and healthcare facilities to efficient public transportation and reliable internet connectivity, you'll find everything you need to feel at home. The country continues to invest in infrastructure development, ensuring a high standard of living for its residents.

A Tropical Paradise with Breathtaking Landscapes

Nature lovers will be captivated by Malaysia's stunning natural beauty. From pristine beaches and lush rainforests to towering mountains and vibrant coral reefs, there's an abundance of outdoor adventures to be had. Whether you enjoy hiking, diving, exploring national parks, or simply relaxing by the sea, Malaysia offers an escape into a tropical paradise.

A Safe and Stable Environment

Malaysia is a politically stable country with a relatively low crime rate. This creates a sense of security and peace of mind for expats, allowing you to focus on enjoying your new life without undue worries about safety. The Malaysian people are known for their friendly and welcoming nature, making it easy to feel comfortable and integrated into the community.

A Growing Economy with Diverse Opportunities

Malaysia has a robust and growing economy, offering diverse opportunities for expats seeking employment or entrepreneurial ventures. The country is a hub for industries such as manufacturing, technology, finance, tourism, and healthcare. With a skilled workforce and a business-friendly environment, Malaysia attracts foreign investment and fosters economic growth.

A Delicious Culinary Journey

Foodies rejoice! Malaysia is a culinary paradise, offering a tantalizing array of flavors and dishes that reflect its multicultural heritage. From spicy Malay curries and aromatic Chinese stir-fries to flavorful Indian dishes and unique indigenous delicacies, there's something to satisfy every palate. Exploring the diverse street food scene and local restaurants is an adventure in itself.

English is Widely Spoken

While the official language of Malaysia is Bahasa Malaysia, English is widely spoken, particularly in urban areas and business settings. This makes it relatively easy for expats to communicate and navigate daily life, reducing the language barrier that can often be a challenge when moving abroad.

A Welcoming and Hospitable Society

Malaysians are known for their warm hospitality and welcoming nature. As an expat, you'll likely experience a sense of community and belonging, making it easier to adapt to your new surroundings. The Malaysian people are generally helpful and friendly, making you feel comfortable and at ease.

A Hub for Education and Healthcare

Malaysia has a well-established education system, offering a range of international schools and universities that cater to expat families. The country is also a growing hub for medical tourism, with high-quality healthcare facilities and skilled medical professionals. This makes Malaysia an attractive destination for families with children and those seeking access to affordable and quality healthcare.

A Relaxed and Laid-Back Lifestyle

If you're seeking a more relaxed and laid-back lifestyle, Malaysia might be the perfect fit. The tropical climate and abundance of natural beauty encourage an outdoor lifestyle, with ample opportunities for recreation and leisure. The pace of life is generally slower than in many Western countries, allowing you to de-stress and enjoy a more balanced way of life.

A Gateway to Travel and Adventure

Malaysia's strategic location and excellent transportation links make it an ideal base for exploring Southeast Asia and beyond. With affordable flights and convenient visa policies, you can easily embark on weekend getaways or extended vacations to neighboring countries. From the ancient temples of Angkor Wat to the bustling streets of Bangkok, there's a world of adventure waiting to be discovered.

In essence, Malaysia offers a unique combination of factors that create a compelling proposition for expats seeking a new and fulfilling life abroad. Whether you're drawn to the cultural diversity, the affordable lifestyle, the natural beauty, or the economic opportunities, Malaysia has something to offer. It's a country where you can embrace new experiences, forge lasting friendships, and create memories that will last a lifetime.

CHAPTER TWO: Visas and Immigration

Navigating the intricacies of visas and immigration is often the first hurdle for anyone planning a move to Malaysia. Fortunately, the Malaysian government has implemented a relatively straightforward system to attract foreign talent and investment. This chapter will guide you through the essential aspects of obtaining the right visa for your circumstances, ensuring a smooth entry into the country.

Understanding the Different Visa Categories

Malaysia offers a range of visa options tailored to suit various purposes of stay, from short-term visits to long-term residency. The type of visa you require will depend on your nationality, the intended duration of your stay, and the nature of your activities in Malaysia.

For short-term stays, most nationalities can enter Malaysia visa-free for tourism or business purposes for periods ranging from 14 to 90 days, depending on your citizenship. You can check the latest visa-free entry requirements on the official website of the Malaysian Immigration Department.

However, if you are planning to stay in Malaysia for an extended period, work, study, or reside permanently, you will need to apply for the appropriate visa before your arrival. Here's a breakdown of the most common visa categories for expats:

- **Employment Pass:** This visa is for foreign professionals who have secured employment with a Malaysian company. It is typically granted for a period of one to five years, depending on your contract.

- **Dependent Pass:** This visa allows spouses and children of Employment Pass holders to join them in Malaysia.

- **Professional Visit Pass:** This visa is for foreign professionals on short-term assignments or consultancy work in Malaysia. It is usually issued for a maximum of 12 months.

- **Student Pass:** This visa is for foreign students enrolled in recognized educational institutions in Malaysia. It is granted for the duration of your studies.

- **Malaysia My Second Home (MM2H):** This program allows foreigners to reside in Malaysia for an extended period, typically 10 years, renewable thereafter. It is a popular option for retirees and those seeking a long-term base in Southeast Asia.

- **Permanent Resident (PR):** This status grants foreigners the right to live and work in Malaysia indefinitely. It is the highest form of immigration status and can lead to Malaysian citizenship in the future.

The Application Process

The visa application process generally involves the following steps:

1. **Identify the appropriate visa category:** Determine the type of visa that best suits your circumstances and intended activities in Malaysia.

2. **Gather the required documents:** The specific documents required will vary depending on the visa category. Commonly required documents include a valid passport, visa application form, recent passport-sized photographs, proof of financial means, and supporting documents such as employment offer letters, educational transcripts, or marriage certificates.

3. **Submit your application:** You can submit your visa application online through the Malaysian Immigration

Department's website, or through a Malaysian embassy or consulate in your home country.

4. **Attend an interview:** Depending on the visa category, you may be required to attend an interview at the embassy or consulate.

5. **Pay the visa fee:** Visa fees vary depending on the visa category and nationality.

6. **Receive your visa:** If your application is approved, you will receive your visa, which will be stamped or affixed to your passport.

Tips for a Smooth Visa Application

To increase your chances of a successful visa application, consider the following tips:

- **Start early:** Begin the application process well in advance of your intended travel date, as processing times can vary.

- **Provide accurate and complete information:** Ensure all the information provided in your application is accurate and up-to-date. Any discrepancies or omissions can delay or jeopardize your application.

- **Meet the financial requirements:** Many visa categories require you to demonstrate sufficient financial means to support yourself during your stay in Malaysia. Provide bank statements, payslips, or other evidence of financial stability.

- **Secure a job offer before applying for an Employment Pass:** Having a job offer from a Malaysian company is a prerequisite for an Employment Pass. Work with your prospective employer to obtain the necessary supporting documents.

- **Enroll in a recognized educational institution for a Student Pass:** Only students enrolled in recognized educational institutions are eligible for a Student Pass. Ensure your chosen institution is accredited and can provide the necessary documentation.
- **Consult with a reputable immigration agent:** If you are unsure about the visa process or need assistance with your application, consider consulting with a reputable immigration agent.

MM2H: A Long-Term Visa for Retirees and Investors

The Malaysia My Second Home (MM2H) program is a popular long-term visa option for retirees, investors, and those seeking a second home in a tropical paradise. Here's a more detailed look at this program:

Eligibility Criteria:

To qualify for the MM2H program, you must meet certain financial and age requirements:

- **Age:** Applicants must be at least 50 years old (or 40 years old for those applying with dependents).
- **Financial Requirements:** Applicants must prove they have sufficient financial means to support themselves during their stay in Malaysia. This can be demonstrated through:
    - **Fixed Deposit:** Applicants must maintain a fixed deposit of RM300,000 (approximately US$65,000) in a Malaysian bank.
    - **Offshore Income:** Applicants must have a monthly offshore income of at least RM10,000 (approximately US$2,170).

Benefits of the MM2H Program:

- **Long-Term Visa:** Successful applicants are granted a 10-year visa, which is renewable thereafter.

- **Multiple Entry:** The visa allows multiple entries and exits from Malaysia, giving you the flexibility to travel freely.

- **Dependent Visa:** Spouses, children under 21 years old, and parents over 60 years old can be included in the visa application.

- **Property Ownership:** MM2H visa holders are allowed to purchase property in Malaysia, subject to certain minimum purchase price requirements.

- **Car Ownership:** MM2H visa holders can purchase and own cars in Malaysia.

- **Tax Benefits:** MM2H visa holders may be eligible for tax exemptions on certain income sources.

Application Process:

The MM2H application process involves:

1. **Submitting an online application:** Applicants can submit their applications online through the official MM2H website.

2. **Providing supporting documents:** Applicants must provide supporting documents such as passport copies, financial statements, and proof of age.

3. **Attending an interview:** Shortlisted applicants may be required to attend an interview at a Malaysian embassy or consulate.

4. **Paying the application fee:** The MM2H application fee is non-refundable.

5. **Receiving a conditional approval letter:** If the application is successful, applicants will receive a conditional approval letter.

6. **Opening a fixed deposit account:** Applicants must open a fixed deposit account in a Malaysian bank and deposit the required amount.

7. **Obtaining a visa:** Upon fulfillment of the financial requirements, applicants will be granted the MM2H visa.

Permanent Residency: The Path to Citizenship

Permanent Residency (PR) in Malaysia is the highest form of immigration status, granting foreigners the right to live and work indefinitely in the country. PR holders enjoy many of the same rights and privileges as Malaysian citizens, with the exception of voting rights and holding public office. PR status can also pave the way for future citizenship.

Eligibility Criteria:

Obtaining PR status in Malaysia is a highly competitive process, with strict eligibility criteria:

- **Length of Stay:** Applicants must have resided in Malaysia for a continuous period of at least five years under a valid visa, such as an Employment Pass or MM2H visa.

- **Investment:** Applicants must make a significant investment in Malaysia, either through business ownership or property purchase.

- **Skills and Qualifications:** Applicants must possess skills and qualifications that are in demand in Malaysia.

- **Clean Criminal Record:** Applicants must have a clean criminal record and good character.

Application Process:

The PR application process involves:

1. **Submitting an application:** Applicants must submit their applications to the Malaysian Immigration Department.

2. **Providing supporting documents:** Applicants must provide extensive supporting documents, including passport copies, visa copies, financial statements, employment records, investment proof, and character references.

3. **Attending an interview:** Shortlisted applicants will be called for an interview with immigration officials.

4. **Receiving a decision:** The processing time for PR applications can be lengthy, often taking several months or even years. Applicants will be notified of the decision in writing.

Obtaining PR status in Malaysia is a significant achievement, granting access to a stable and prosperous future in the country.

CHAPTER THREE: Finding a Place to Live

So, you've decided to take the plunge and move to Malaysia! That's exciting! Now, the big question arises: where should you set up your new home? Malaysia offers a diverse range of living options, from bustling city centers to serene suburbs and idyllic coastal towns. The best choice for you will depend on your personal preferences, lifestyle, budget, and whether you're moving solo, as a couple, or with your family. This chapter will guide you through the key considerations to help you find the perfect neighborhood in Malaysia that feels just right.

Understanding the Lay of the Land

Before diving into specific neighborhoods, it's helpful to get a sense of Malaysia's geography and its key urban centers. As you know by now, Malaysia is divided into two main regions: Peninsular Malaysia and East Malaysia (Malaysian Borneo).

Peninsular Malaysia is home to the country's capital, Kuala Lumpur, and other major cities like Penang and Johor Bahru. It is the more developed region, with excellent infrastructure, a wide range of amenities, and a cosmopolitan vibe.

East Malaysia, comprising the states of Sabah and Sarawak, offers a more laid-back lifestyle, closer to nature. It boasts stunning rainforests, pristine beaches, and unique indigenous cultures.

Kuala Lumpur: The Vibrant Capital

Kuala Lumpur, often referred to as KL, is the beating heart of Malaysia, pulsating with energy, diversity, and a blend of modern skyscrapers and historic charm. It's a city that never sleeps, offering an array of entertainment, dining, and shopping options.

For expats, KL offers a familiar cosmopolitan experience, with a large international community, making it easier to adjust to a new environment. However, the fast-paced city life can also be overwhelming for some.

Here are some of the popular expat neighborhoods in KL:

- **Mont Kiara:** Known for its upscale condominiums, international schools, and family-friendly atmosphere, Mont Kiara is a favorite among expats with families. It boasts a good mix of restaurants, cafes, and convenience stores, creating a self-contained community.

- **Bangsar:** A vibrant suburb with a bohemian vibe, Bangsar offers trendy cafes, bars, restaurants, and independent boutiques. It attracts a mix of young professionals, expats, and locals, creating a lively social scene.

- **Taman Tun Dr Ismail (TTDI):** A leafy suburb with a more laid-back feel, TTDI offers spacious landed properties, green parks, and a good selection of local eateries and shops. It's a popular choice for families seeking a quieter environment while still being relatively close to the city center.

- **Ampang:** Located east of KL's city center, Ampang offers a mix of high-rise condominiums, international schools, and embassies. It's a popular choice for diplomats and expats working in the surrounding area.

- **KLCC (Kuala Lumpur City Centre):** This is the heart of KL's business district, home to the iconic Petronas Twin Towers and a plethora of upscale shopping malls, hotels, and restaurants. It's a convenient location for those working in the city center, but can be quite expensive.

Penang: The Pearl of the Orient

Penang, an island state off the northwest coast of Peninsular Malaysia, is renowned for its colonial heritage, vibrant street art scene, and delectable street food. It offers a more relaxed pace of life compared to KL, with a unique blend of old-world charm and modern amenities.

Here are some popular expat neighborhoods in Penang:

- **George Town:** The capital of Penang, George Town is a UNESCO World Heritage site, with a captivating mix of colonial architecture, traditional shophouses, street art, and a thriving culinary scene. It attracts a mix of artists, expats, and tourists, creating a vibrant and multicultural atmosphere.

- **Batu Ferringhi:** A popular beach destination on the north coast of Penang, Batu Ferringhi offers a range of resorts, hotels, restaurants, and watersports activities. It's a great option for those seeking a beachside lifestyle.

- **Tanjung Bungah:** A coastal suburb with a mix of high-rise condominiums, landed properties, and seafront views, Tanjung Bungah offers a more tranquil environment compared to Batu Ferringhi. It's a popular choice for families and retirees seeking a peaceful coastal lifestyle.

Johor Bahru: The Gateway to Singapore

Johor Bahru, the southernmost city in Peninsular Malaysia, is a bustling economic hub and a popular choice for expats working in neighboring Singapore. It offers lower living costs compared to Singapore, making it an attractive option for those seeking affordability and convenience.

Here are some popular expat neighborhoods in Johor Bahru:

- **Iskandar Puteri:** A rapidly developing zone in Johor Bahru, Iskandar Puteri offers a range of modern amenities, including shopping malls, theme parks, international schools, and healthcare facilities. It's a popular choice for families seeking a well-planned community.

- **Nusajaya:** Another planned development in Iskandar Puteri, Nusajaya offers a mix of residential, commercial, and educational facilities, with a focus on sustainability and green living.
- **Johor Bahru City Centre:** The heart of Johor Bahru's business district, the city center offers a range of shopping malls, hotels, and restaurants. It's a convenient location for those working in the city, but can be quite crowded.

East Malaysia: Sabah and Sarawak

East Malaysia, encompassing the states of Sabah and Sarawak on the island of Borneo, offers a more adventurous and nature-oriented lifestyle. It boasts stunning rainforests, pristine beaches, and unique indigenous cultures. However, East Malaysia is less developed than Peninsular Malaysia, with limited infrastructure and amenities in some areas.

Here are some popular expat destinations in East Malaysia:

- **Kota Kinabalu (Sabah):** The capital of Sabah, Kota Kinabalu is a vibrant city with a stunning coastal setting. It offers a mix of modern amenities, cultural attractions, and access to nearby islands and national parks.
- **Kuching (Sarawak):** The capital of Sarawak, Kuching is a charming city with a rich history and a laid-back atmosphere. It offers a blend of colonial architecture, cultural heritage sites, and access to nearby rainforests and national parks.

Choosing the Right Neighborhood for You

With so many diverse living options in Malaysia, finding the right neighborhood for your needs and preferences is essential. Here are some key factors to consider:

- **Lifestyle:** Are you seeking a bustling city life with endless entertainment options, a tranquil suburban lifestyle with green spaces and family-friendly amenities, or a laid-back coastal lifestyle with beach access and watersports activities?

- **Budget:** Housing costs can vary significantly across different neighborhoods in Malaysia. Determine your budget and explore neighborhoods that align with your affordability.

- **Commute:** If you're working in Malaysia, consider the proximity of your chosen neighborhood to your workplace and the available transportation options. Traffic congestion can be a significant factor in major cities like KL.

- **Family Needs:** If you're moving with children, prioritize neighborhoods with good schools, parks, and family-friendly amenities.

- **Culture and Community:** Malaysia's diverse ethnicities offer a unique cultural experience. Explore neighborhoods that align with your cultural interests and preferences, whether you're seeking a predominantly Malay, Chinese, Indian, or international community.

- **Amenities and Infrastructure:** Consider the availability of essential amenities, such as supermarkets, healthcare facilities, banks, and transportation options in your chosen neighborhood.

- **Safety and Security:** Malaysia is generally a safe country, but crime rates can vary across different areas. Research the safety and security of neighborhoods you're considering.

Finding Your New Home: Resources and Tips

Once you've identified neighborhoods that pique your interest, the next step is to find a suitable home. Here are some valuable resources and tips to aid your search:

- **Online Property Portals:** Websites like PropertyGuru, iProperty, and Mudah.my are popular online portals for finding properties for rent or sale in Malaysia. You can filter your search by location, price, property type, and other criteria.

- **Real Estate Agents:** Consider working with a reputable real estate agent who can help you navigate the local property market, negotiate prices, and handle the paperwork involved in renting or buying a property.

- **Word of Mouth:** Networking with other expats and locals can be a valuable way to get insider information on neighborhoods, available properties, and reliable real estate agents.

- **Visit Potential Neighborhoods:** Once you've shortlisted potential neighborhoods, take the time to visit them in person. Explore the area, check out local amenities, and get a feel for the community vibe.

- **Consider Short-Term Rentals:** If you're unsure about a particular neighborhood, consider renting a property for a short term before committing to a long-term lease or purchase. This will give you a chance to experience the area firsthand and make an informed decision.

Understanding Rental Agreements and Property Purchase

Whether you're renting or buying a property in Malaysia, it's crucial to understand the legal aspects involved:

Rental Agreements:

- **Tenancy Agreement:** A tenancy agreement is a legal contract between the landlord and tenant, outlining the terms of the rental, including the rental amount, duration of the lease, and responsibilities of both parties.

- **Security Deposit:** Landlords typically require a security deposit, usually equivalent to two to three months' rent, which is refundable at the end of the lease, subject to deductions for any damages or unpaid rent.

- **Utilities:** Clarify whether utilities are included in the rent or if you'll be responsible for paying them separately.

Property Purchase:

- **Sale and Purchase Agreement (SPA):** The SPA is a legal document that outlines the terms of the property purchase, including the purchase price, payment schedule, and legal obligations of both the buyer and seller.

- **Legal Fees:** Property purchase in Malaysia involves various legal fees, including stamp duty, legal fees for drafting the SPA, and registration fees.

- **Foreign Ownership:** Foreigners are generally allowed to purchase property in Malaysia, but there are certain restrictions, such as minimum purchase price requirements, that vary depending on the type of property and location.

Making Your Move to Malaysia

Finding a place to live is a crucial step in your relocation journey to Malaysia. By considering your lifestyle, budget, and priorities, and utilizing available resources, you'll be well on your way to finding a neighborhood that feels like home. Once you've secured your new abode, you can start settling in and embracing the vibrant and multicultural experience that awaits you in Malaysia.

CHAPTER FOUR: The Cost of Living in Malaysia

One of the biggest draws for many expats considering a move to Malaysia is the relatively low cost of living. While the exact expenses will naturally vary depending on your lifestyle choices, desired level of comfort, and location within the country, you'll generally find that your budget goes further in Malaysia compared to many Western countries. This chapter will provide a comprehensive overview of the typical expenses you can expect as an expat in Malaysia, helping you plan your finances and make informed decisions.

Housing: A Wide Range of Options for Every Budget

Housing is typically the largest expense for most expats, and thankfully Malaysia offers a wide range of options to suit various budgets and preferences. Whether you're looking for a modern high-rise condominium in a bustling city center, a spacious landed property in a leafy suburb, or a charming townhouse in a historic neighborhood, you'll find plenty of choices.

Rental costs can vary significantly depending on the location, property type, size, and amenities. In general, rental rates are lower in smaller towns and suburban areas compared to major cities like Kuala Lumpur and Penang.

For a one-bedroom apartment in a decent neighborhood outside the city center, you can expect to pay around RM1,500 to RM2,500 per month. A three-bedroom condominium in a more upscale area could cost anywhere from RM3,000 to RM6,000 per month. If you're looking for a luxurious villa or bungalow, be prepared to pay upwards of RM10,000 per month.

Utilities, such as electricity, water, and gas, are generally affordable in Malaysia. For a typical apartment, you can expect to pay around RM200 to RM400 per month for utilities.

Food: A Gastronomic Adventure at Affordable Prices

Malaysia is a food lover's paradise, offering a tantalizing array of flavors and cuisines at remarkably affordable prices. From hawker stalls and food courts to local restaurants and fine dining establishments, you'll find an abundance of options to satisfy every palate and budget.

One of the joys of living in Malaysia is the vibrant street food scene. You can enjoy a delicious meal of nasi lemak (coconut rice with various accompaniments) for as little as RM5, or a hearty bowl of laksa (spicy noodle soup) for around RM8. At local restaurants, you can find a wide range of dishes, including Malay, Chinese, Indian, and international cuisines, for around RM15 to RM30 per meal.

If you prefer to cook at home, groceries are also relatively affordable in Malaysia. Fresh produce, meats, and seafood are readily available at local markets and supermarkets. You can expect to spend around RM500 to RM1,000 per month on groceries for a couple, depending on your dietary habits.

Transportation: Getting Around Efficiently and Affordably

Malaysia boasts an efficient and affordable transportation system, making it easy to get around the country. Public transportation, including buses, trains, and light rail transit (LRT), is widely available in major cities and towns. A single bus or train ride typically costs RM1 to RM3, depending on the distance.

Taxis and ride-hailing services like Grab are also readily available, providing convenient door-to-door transportation. A short taxi ride within the city center might cost around RM10 to RM20, while a longer journey to the suburbs could cost RM30 to RM50.

If you prefer to drive, car ownership is relatively affordable in Malaysia compared to some other countries. However, traffic congestion can be a significant issue in major cities, especially during peak hours. Petrol prices are also subsidized by the government, making it relatively affordable to fuel your vehicle.

Healthcare: Quality and Affordable Medical Services

Malaysia has a two-tier healthcare system, with both public and private options available. The public healthcare system is heavily subsidized by the government, making it accessible and affordable for all Malaysians. Expats are also eligible for public healthcare services, although they may pay higher fees than Malaysian citizens.

Private healthcare facilities in Malaysia offer a higher standard of care, with shorter waiting times, more modern equipment, and a wider range of specialists. However, private healthcare can be significantly more expensive than public healthcare.

It's advisable for expats to have private health insurance to cover the costs of private healthcare services. The cost of health insurance will vary depending on your age, health condition, and the level of coverage you choose.

Education: International Schools and Local Options

For expat families with children, education is an important consideration. Malaysia offers a range of schooling options, including international schools, private schools, and public schools.

International schools in Malaysia follow international curricula, such as the International Baccalaureate (IB) or the British curriculum. They typically provide a high standard of education and cater to a diverse student body, but they also come with higher tuition fees. Annual tuition fees for international schools can range from RM20,000 to RM60,000 per year, depending on the school and grade level.

Private schools in Malaysia follow the Malaysian national curriculum but offer a more personalized learning environment and smaller class sizes. Tuition fees for private schools are generally lower than international schools, ranging from RM5,000 to RM20,000 per year.

Public schools in Malaysia are free for Malaysian citizens, but expats may be required to pay tuition fees. Public schools follow the Malaysian national curriculum and are generally taught in Bahasa Malaysia.

Entertainment and Leisure: Affordable Options for Fun and Relaxation

Malaysia offers a diverse range of entertainment and leisure options to suit every taste and budget. From shopping malls and cinemas to theme parks and outdoor activities, there's no shortage of things to do.

Movie tickets typically cost around RM15 to RM25, while a meal at a casual restaurant could cost RM20 to RM40 per person. Tickets to theme parks and other attractions can range from RM50 to RM150 per person.

Other Expenses: From Mobile Phones to Housekeeping

Besides the major expenses mentioned above, here's a breakdown of other typical costs you can expect in Malaysia:

- **Mobile Phone Plans:** Mobile phone plans in Malaysia are generally affordable, with a variety of prepaid and postpaid options available. You can get a decent mobile phone plan with data, calls, and SMS for around RM50 to RM100 per month.

- **Internet:** Broadband internet access is readily available in Malaysia, with speeds and prices varying depending on the provider and plan. You can expect to pay around RM80 to RM150 per month for a reliable broadband internet connection.

- **Domestic Help:** Hiring a domestic helper, such as a maid or cleaner, is common in Malaysia. The cost of domestic help can range from RM800 to RM1,500 per month, depending on the experience and duties of the helper.

- **Personal Care:** Haircuts, beauty treatments, and other personal care services are generally affordable in Malaysia. A haircut at a local salon might cost around RM20 to RM50.

Overall Cost of Living: A Comfortable Lifestyle within Reach

The overall cost of living in Malaysia is relatively affordable, allowing expats to enjoy a comfortable lifestyle without breaking the bank. While costs can vary depending on your lifestyle choices and location, here's a rough estimate of monthly expenses for a couple living in a mid-range neighborhood in Kuala Lumpur:

Expense Category	Estimated Monthly Cost (RM)
Housing (2-bedroom apartment)	3,000
Utilities	300
Food	1,500
Transportation	500
Entertainment	500
Healthcare (insurance)	500
Mobile Phone	100
Internet	100
Other Expenses	500
Total Estimated Monthly Expenses	**6,500**

Of course, these are just estimates, and your actual expenses may be higher or lower depending on your individual circumstances and choices. However, this provides a general idea of what to expect.

Tips for Managing Your Expenses in Malaysia

Here are some tips for managing your expenses and making your money go further in Malaysia:

- **Negotiate Rental Rates:** Don't be afraid to negotiate rental rates with landlords, especially if you're signing a long-term lease.

- **Embrace the Local Food Scene:** Eating at local hawker stalls and food courts is significantly cheaper than dining at restaurants.

- **Utilize Public Transportation:** Public transportation in Malaysia is efficient and affordable, and it can help you avoid the costs and hassles of car ownership, especially in congested cities.

- **Shop Around for Groceries:** Compare prices at different supermarkets and local markets to find the best deals on groceries.

- **Take Advantage of Free Activities:** Malaysia offers plenty of free activities and attractions, such as parks, beaches, and museums.

- **Learn to Bargain:** Bargaining is a common practice in Malaysia, especially at local markets and street stalls. Don't be shy to haggle for a better price.

Malaysia's affordability, combined with its vibrant culture, modern amenities, and stunning natural beauty, makes it an attractive destination for expats seeking a high quality of life without the high cost of living. With careful planning and a willingness to embrace the local lifestyle, you can enjoy a comfortable and fulfilling life in Malaysia.

CHAPTER FIVE: Healthcare in Malaysia

For many expats, the quality and accessibility of healthcare are major considerations when choosing a new home. Fortunately, Malaysia boasts a well-developed healthcare system that is often lauded for its quality, affordability, and efficiency. This chapter will provide a comprehensive overview of the healthcare landscape in Malaysia, covering everything from the structure of the system to the types of facilities available, the costs involved, and essential tips for expats to navigate their healthcare needs in the country.

A Dual System: Public and Private Healthcare

Malaysia operates a dual healthcare system, consisting of both public and private sectors. This two-tiered approach offers a range of choices to suit different needs and budgets, providing access to quality healthcare for all.

Public Healthcare: Accessible and Affordable

The public healthcare system in Malaysia is heavily subsidized by the government, making it accessible and affordable for all Malaysian citizens. Expats are also eligible for public healthcare services, although they may pay slightly higher fees than citizens.

The public healthcare system comprises a network of government-funded hospitals and clinics, providing a wide range of medical services, from general consultations to specialized treatments. While the quality of care in public facilities is generally good, waiting times can be long, particularly for non-emergency procedures.

Private Healthcare: Quality Care and Shorter Waiting Times

The private healthcare sector in Malaysia offers a higher standard of care, with modern facilities, advanced equipment, and a wider range of specialized medical professionals. Private hospitals and clinics often provide shorter waiting times, personalized services, and a more comfortable environment compared to public facilities.

However, private healthcare comes at a premium, with costs significantly higher than in the public sector. Expats are strongly advised to have private health insurance to cover the costs of private healthcare services.

Navigating the Healthcare System: Key Considerations for Expats

As an expat, navigating the healthcare system in Malaysia may initially seem daunting, but with a bit of understanding and preparation, you can easily access the care you need. Here are some key considerations:

Choosing a Healthcare Provider

When choosing a healthcare provider, whether it's a general practitioner (GP), a specialist, or a hospital, it's essential to consider factors such as:

- **Location:** Choose a provider that is conveniently located and easily accessible from your home or workplace.

- **Reputation and Accreditation:** Research the reputation and accreditation of healthcare providers to ensure they meet high standards of quality and safety.

- **Specialization:** If you require specialized medical care, look for providers with expertise in the specific field.

- **Language:** While many doctors and medical professionals in Malaysia speak English, particularly in private facilities, it's helpful to inquire about language proficiency if you have specific communication needs.

- **Insurance Coverage:** Check with your health insurance provider to confirm which healthcare providers are covered under your plan.

Understanding Health Insurance

Having comprehensive health insurance is crucial for expats in Malaysia, as it provides financial protection against the potentially high costs of private healthcare services. When choosing a health insurance plan, consider the following factors:

- **Coverage:** Ensure the plan covers a wide range of medical services, including hospitalization, surgery, specialist consultations, and emergency medical evacuation.

- **Deductibles and Co-payments:** Understand the deductibles and co-payments associated with the plan, which are the amounts you'll need to pay out of pocket before the insurance coverage kicks in.

- **Network of Providers:** Check if the insurance plan has a network of healthcare providers, and if your preferred providers are included in the network.

- **Premiums:** Compare premiums from different insurance providers to find a plan that fits your budget and needs.

Registering for Public Healthcare

If you're eligible for public healthcare services, you can register at a government clinic or hospital. You'll need to provide your passport, visa, and other relevant documents for registration. Once registered, you'll receive a health card that you can use to access subsidized medical services at public facilities.

Common Ailments and Health Concerns

Malaysia's tropical climate and diverse environment can pose some unique health challenges for expats. Here are some common ailments and health concerns to be aware of:

- **Dengue Fever:** This mosquito-borne viral disease is prevalent in Malaysia, particularly during the rainy season. Symptoms include high fever, headache, muscle and joint pain, and rash. It's crucial to take precautions to prevent mosquito bites, such as using insect repellent, wearing long sleeves and pants, and eliminating mosquito breeding grounds.

- **Foodborne Illnesses:** Food poisoning can occur due to consuming contaminated food or water. It's essential to practice good food hygiene, such as washing hands before meals, choosing reputable eateries, and avoiding raw or undercooked food.

- **Heatstroke and Dehydration:** The hot and humid weather in Malaysia can lead to heatstroke and dehydration. Stay hydrated by drinking plenty of water, avoid strenuous activities during the hottest part of the day, and wear light, loose-fitting clothing.

- **Respiratory Infections:** Air pollution can be a concern in some Malaysian cities, potentially aggravating respiratory conditions. Consider wearing a mask in polluted areas, particularly if you have asthma or other respiratory issues.

Vaccinations and Health Precautions

Before moving to Malaysia, it's advisable to consult with your doctor or a travel health clinic to ensure you are up-to-date on vaccinations and receive necessary health advice. Recommended vaccinations may include:

- Hepatitis A and B

- Typhoid

- Tetanus-Diphtheria-Pertussis

- Measles-Mumps-Rubella (MMR)

- Japanese Encephalitis (for those spending extended time in rural areas)

It's also advisable to pack a basic first-aid kit and any essential medications you require.

Medical Emergencies: How to Seek Immediate Assistance

In case of a medical emergency, you can dial 999 for an ambulance. Ambulance services in Malaysia are generally efficient and responsive, particularly in urban areas. You can also call your health insurance provider's emergency hotline for assistance and guidance.

Pharmacies and Over-the-Counter Medications

Pharmacies are widely available in Malaysia, offering a range of over-the-counter medications, vitamins, and supplements. You can usually find common medications without a prescription, although it's always advisable to consult with a doctor or pharmacist before taking any new medications.

Traditional and Alternative Medicine

Traditional and alternative medicine practices, such as Traditional Chinese Medicine (TCM) and Ayurvedic medicine, are also prevalent in Malaysia. These practices offer a holistic approach to health and well-being, with treatments ranging from herbal remedies to acupuncture and massage therapy.

Tips for Staying Healthy in Malaysia

Maintaining good health in Malaysia involves taking proactive steps to prevent illnesses and manage your well-being. Here are some essential tips:

- **Stay Hydrated:** Drink plenty of water throughout the day, especially in hot weather.

- **Eat a Balanced Diet:** Enjoy Malaysia's diverse cuisine, but maintain a balanced diet with plenty of fruits, vegetables, and whole grains.

- **Exercise Regularly:** Find ways to incorporate regular exercise into your routine, whether it's walking, jogging, swimming, or joining a gym.

- **Practice Good Hygiene:** Wash your hands frequently, particularly before meals and after using the toilet.

- **Prevent Mosquito Bites:** Use insect repellent, wear long sleeves and pants, and eliminate mosquito breeding grounds around your home.

- **Manage Stress:** Find healthy ways to manage stress, such as yoga, meditation, or spending time in nature.

- **Get Regular Check-ups:** Schedule regular check-ups with your doctor to monitor your health and detect any potential issues early on.

Finding Reliable Healthcare Information

If you're seeking reliable healthcare information in Malaysia, here are some helpful resources:

- **Ministry of Health Malaysia:** The Ministry of Health's website provides comprehensive information on healthcare services, facilities, and regulations in Malaysia.

- **Malaysian Medical Association (MMA):** The MMA is a professional body representing doctors in Malaysia. Their website provides information on healthcare professionals, medical ethics, and public health issues.

- **Private Hospitals and Clinics:** Most private hospitals and clinics have websites that provide information on their services, specialists, and contact details.

- **Expat Forums and Groups:** Online forums and social media groups for expats in Malaysia can be valuable sources of information and recommendations for healthcare providers.

Malaysia's robust healthcare system provides expats with access to quality medical services, from affordable public healthcare to high-end private facilities. By understanding the structure of the system, choosing the right healthcare providers, having comprehensive health insurance, and taking preventive measures, you can ensure your health and well-being are well taken care of in your new home.

CHAPTER SIX: Education: Options for Expat Families

For expat families moving to Malaysia, securing a quality education for their children is a top priority. Thankfully, Malaysia offers a diverse and well-regarded education system with a range of options to cater to different needs, preferences, and budgets. This chapter will explore the various schooling choices available to expat families, from prestigious international schools following globally recognized curricula to private schools offering a more personalized learning environment and public schools providing a local experience. We'll delve into the different curricula, admission procedures, fee structures, and key considerations to help you make the best educational choices for your children.

International Schools: A Global Standard of Education

International schools in Malaysia have gained immense popularity among expat families for several compelling reasons. These schools typically offer a high standard of education, internationally recognized curricula, a diverse student body, and a supportive environment that eases the transition for expat children.

Curricula and Accreditation

International schools in Malaysia typically follow globally recognized curricula, such as:

- **International Baccalaureate (IB):** The IB program is renowned for its holistic approach to education, fostering critical thinking, intercultural understanding, and a lifelong love of learning. It is offered at various levels, from Primary Years Programme (PYP) to Diploma Programme (DP).

- **British Curriculum:** Schools following the British curriculum prepare students for the IGCSE (International

General Certificate of Secondary Education) and A-Level examinations, widely recognized for university admission in the UK and other countries.

- **American Curriculum:** Some international schools offer the American curriculum, culminating in the SAT (Scholastic Assessment Test) or ACT (American College Testing) examinations, widely accepted for university admissions in the US.

Accreditation is another crucial factor to consider when choosing an international school. Accrediting bodies ensure that schools meet specific quality standards and maintain academic rigor. Reputable accrediting organizations include the Council of International Schools (CIS) and the Western Association of Schools and Colleges (WASC).

Admissions and Fees

Admission procedures vary among international schools, but generally involve:

1. **Application Form:** Submit an application form along with supporting documents, such as the child's previous school records, passport copies, and visa details.

2. **Entrance Assessment:** Most international schools conduct entrance assessments to evaluate the child's academic abilities and suitability for the program.

3. **Interview:** An interview with the admissions team and possibly the principal may be required to assess the child's personality, interests, and overall fit with the school's culture.

Tuition fees for international schools are considerably higher than those of private or public schools, reflecting the high standard of education, facilities, and resources they offer. Annual fees can vary widely depending on the school, grade level, and curriculum.

In general, expect to pay anywhere from RM20,000 to RM60,000 per year for primary school and up to RM80,000 per year for secondary school.

Advantages of International Schools

- **High-Quality Education:** International schools are known for their rigorous academic programs, experienced teachers, and excellent facilities, providing a strong foundation for future success.

- **Globally Recognized Curricula:** The internationally recognized curricula offered at these schools ensure that students can seamlessly transition to other international schools or universities worldwide.

- **Diverse Student Body:** International schools attract students from various nationalities, creating a multicultural and enriching learning environment that fosters intercultural understanding and global citizenship.

- **Strong Support System:** Many international schools have dedicated support staff, such as counselors and learning support specialists, to assist expat children with their academic and social-emotional well-being.

Disadvantages of International Schools

- **High Tuition Fees:** The main drawback of international schools is the high tuition fees, which can be a significant financial consideration for expat families.

- **Limited Exposure to Local Culture:** While the multicultural environment of international schools is a plus, it may also limit exposure to the local Malaysian culture.

Private Schools: A Personalized Learning Experience

Private schools in Malaysia offer an alternative to international schools, providing a more personalized learning experience and a focus on the Malaysian national curriculum. They are a popular choice for Malaysian families seeking a more focused educational environment and for expat families who want their children to experience the local education system.

Curriculum and Language

Private schools in Malaysia follow the Malaysian national curriculum, which is set by the Ministry of Education. The curriculum emphasizes core subjects like Bahasa Malaysia (Malay language), English, Mathematics, Science, and Islamic Studies (for Muslim students).

The main language of instruction in private schools is Bahasa Malaysia, but many schools also offer English as a second language. Some private schools may also have bilingual programs where certain subjects are taught in English.

Admissions and Fees

Admission procedures for private schools typically involve:

1. **Application Form:** Submit an application form along with supporting documents, such as the child's birth certificate, previous school records, and passport copies.

2. **Entrance Assessment:** Some private schools conduct entrance assessments to evaluate the child's academic abilities.

3. **Interview:** An interview with the admissions team or principal may be required.

Tuition fees for private schools are generally lower than those of international schools, but they can still vary significantly depending on the school's location, reputation, and facilities.

Expect to pay anywhere from RM5,000 to RM20,000 per year for primary and secondary school.

Advantages of Private Schools

- **Personalized Learning Environment:** Private schools often have smaller class sizes than public schools, allowing for more individualized attention from teachers and a more personalized learning experience.

- **Focus on Malaysian Curriculum:** Private schools provide a strong foundation in the Malaysian national curriculum, which can be beneficial for expat children who plan to stay in Malaysia long-term.

- **Stronger Emphasis on Language Development:** With Bahasa Malaysia as the primary language of instruction, private schools can provide a more immersive environment for language acquisition.

Disadvantages of Private Schools

- **Less Curriculum Flexibility:** The focus on the national curriculum may limit flexibility in terms of subject choices and learning styles.

- **Language Barrier:** The primary use of Bahasa Malaysia may pose a challenge for expat children who are not yet proficient in the language.

Public Schools: A Local Experience

Public schools in Malaysia are government-funded and offer free education to all Malaysian citizens. While expat children are generally not eligible for free education in public schools, they can enroll by paying tuition fees.

Curriculum and Language

Public schools follow the Malaysian national curriculum, with Bahasa Malaysia as the main language of instruction. The curriculum is standardized across the country, ensuring consistency in education.

Admissions and Fees

Admission to public schools is based on a catchment area system, where priority is given to children residing within a specific geographical zone. Expat children may face challenges securing admission to public schools, particularly in highly sought-after areas.

Tuition fees for expat children in public schools are nominal compared to international and private schools. However, the language barrier and differences in curriculum may make public schools a less suitable option for many expat families.

Advantages of Public Schools

- **Affordable Education:** Public schools provide an affordable education option for expat families.

- **Immersion in Local Culture:** Enrolling in a public school provides a unique opportunity for expat children to fully immerse themselves in the local Malaysian culture and language.

Disadvantages of Public Schools

- **Language Barrier:** The primary use of Bahasa Malaysia can be a significant barrier for expat children who are not yet proficient in the language.

- **Different Curriculum:** The Malaysian national curriculum may differ significantly from the curriculum your child is accustomed to, potentially leading to challenges in transitioning back to their home country's education system in the future.

- **Limited Resources:** Public schools often have limited resources and larger class sizes compared to international or private schools.

Other Educational Options: Homeschooling and Special Needs Education

Besides the mainstream schooling options, Malaysia also offers:

- **Homeschooling:** Homeschooling is a legal option in Malaysia, allowing parents to provide their children with education at home. There are homeschooling support groups and resources available for parents who choose this option.

- **Special Needs Education:** Malaysia has a growing number of schools and centers catering to children with special needs. These institutions provide specialized programs and support services to meet the unique learning requirements of these students.

Choosing the Right School: Key Considerations

Selecting the best school for your child is a significant decision, and there's no one-size-fits-all answer. Consider these key factors:

- **Child's Age and Learning Style:** Consider your child's age, learning style, and academic abilities when choosing a school. Some schools are better suited to certain learning styles or age groups.

- **Curriculum and Language:** Determine which curriculum and language of instruction best align with your child's needs and future educational goals.

- **Location and Commute:** Choose a school that is conveniently located and easily accessible from your home. Factor in the daily commute and traffic conditions.

- **School Culture and Values:** Research the school's culture, values, and extracurricular activities to ensure they align with your family's priorities.

- **Budget:** Consider your budget and explore schools that offer tuition fees within your affordability.

- **Class Size and Teacher-Student Ratio:** Smaller class sizes and a lower teacher-student ratio often allow for more personalized attention and support for students.

- **Facilities and Resources:** Assess the school's facilities, resources, and technology to ensure they meet your expectations.

- **Reputation and Accreditation:** Research the school's reputation, accreditation, and academic track record.

Application Timeline and Deadlines

International and private schools typically have specific application timelines and deadlines. It's crucial to start the application process well in advance of your planned move to Malaysia to secure a place for your child. Contact the schools directly to inquire about their specific application procedures and deadlines.

Preparing for Transition: Easing Your Child's Adjustment

Moving to a new country and starting a new school can be a significant adjustment for children. Here are some tips to help ease the transition:

- **Involve Your Child in the Decision:** If possible, involve your child in the school selection process, allowing them to visit potential schools and express their preferences.

- **Communicate Openly:** Talk to your child about their feelings and concerns about the move and the new school. Address their anxieties and provide reassurance.

- **Connect with Other Expat Families:** Networking with other expat families can provide valuable support and a sense of community for your child.

- **Encourage Extracurricular Activities:** Joining clubs, sports teams, or other extracurricular activities can help your child make new friends, develop their interests, and integrate into the school community.

- **Be Patient and Supportive:** Adjusting to a new school takes time. Be patient and supportive of your child as they navigate this transition.

Securing a quality education for your children is a crucial step in ensuring a successful relocation to Malaysia. By carefully considering the various schooling options, understanding the curricula, fees, and admission procedures, and preparing for the transition, you can set your children up for success in their new educational journey. With a supportive environment and a commitment to learning, your children can thrive academically and personally in Malaysia's diverse and welcoming educational landscape.

CHAPTER SEVEN: Working in Malaysia: Job Market and Business Opportunities

Malaysia, with its burgeoning economy and strategic location in the heart of Southeast Asia, presents a promising landscape for expats seeking new career paths or entrepreneurial ventures. This chapter will delve into the intricacies of the Malaysian job market, exploring the in-demand industries, visa requirements for working professionals, salary expectations, and the overall work culture. We'll also touch upon the opportunities for setting up a business in Malaysia, highlighting the government initiatives, incentives, and resources available to support foreign entrepreneurs.

A Thriving Economy with Diverse Opportunities

Malaysia's economy has transformed significantly over the past few decades, shifting from a reliance on agriculture and natural resources to a more diversified and knowledge-based economy. The country has emerged as a hub for several key industries, including manufacturing, technology, finance, tourism, and healthcare, offering a wide range of opportunities for skilled professionals.

In-Demand Industries: Where the Jobs Are

The Malaysian government has actively promoted the growth of key industries through various initiatives and incentives, creating a favorable environment for both local and foreign investment. As an expat seeking employment in Malaysia, it's beneficial to target industries with high demand for skilled labor.

Here are some of the sectors with promising job prospects for expats:

- **Oil and Gas:** Malaysia is a major producer and exporter of oil and gas, with a well-established industry supported by the national oil company, Petronas. The sector offers opportunities for engineers, geologists, technicians, and other specialized professionals.

- **Information Technology (IT):** The IT sector in Malaysia is rapidly growing, driven by the government's push towards a digital economy. There's a high demand for software developers, data analysts, cybersecurity experts, and other IT professionals.

- **Finance and Banking:** Kuala Lumpur is a major financial hub in Southeast Asia, home to a large number of banks, financial institutions, and insurance companies. The sector offers opportunities for financial analysts, accountants, investment bankers, and other finance professionals.

- **Manufacturing:** Malaysia is a manufacturing powerhouse, particularly in the electronics, electrical appliances, and automotive industries. The sector requires skilled engineers, technicians, production managers, and quality control specialists.

- **Tourism and Hospitality:** Malaysia's tourism industry is a major contributor to the economy, with a diverse range of attractions, from pristine beaches and lush rainforests to cultural heritage sites and bustling cities. The sector offers opportunities for hotel managers, tour guides, chefs, and other hospitality professionals.

- **Healthcare:** Malaysia is a growing hub for medical tourism, attracting patients from around the region with its affordable and high-quality healthcare services. The sector needs doctors, nurses, pharmacists, and other healthcare professionals.

Employment Pass: The Key to Working in Malaysia

For most expats seeking employment in Malaysia, obtaining an Employment Pass (EP) is essential. This visa allows foreign professionals to work in the country for a specified period, typically one to five years, depending on the employment contract.

Eligibility Criteria: Meeting the Requirements

To qualify for an EP, you must meet certain criteria:

- **Job Offer:** You must have a valid job offer from a registered Malaysian company.

- **Minimum Salary:** The Malaysian government has set a minimum salary requirement for EP applicants, which varies depending on the industry, job role, and experience level.

- **Qualifications and Experience:** Your qualifications and experience must be relevant to the job offer and meet the requirements set by the employer and the Immigration Department.

- **Company Quota:** Employers in Malaysia are subject to quotas for hiring foreign workers. Your employer must have a quota available to sponsor your EP application.

Application Process: Step by Step

The EP application process typically involves the following steps:

1. **Employer Application:** Your prospective employer must first submit an application on your behalf to the Expatriate Services Division (ESD) of the Immigration Department.

2. **Supporting Documents:** Your employer will need to provide supporting documents, including the company's business registration details, your employment contract, and proof of your qualifications and experience.

3. **Processing Time:** The processing time for EP applications can vary, but typically takes around four to six weeks.

4. **Visa Issuance:** If your application is approved, you will receive a notification, and the EP will be endorsed on your passport.

Salary Expectations: What You Can Earn

Salaries for expats in Malaysia vary widely depending on the industry, job role, experience level, and nationality. However, in general, salaries for skilled professionals are competitive, particularly in the oil and gas, IT, and finance sectors.

It's important to negotiate a salary package that commensurate with your qualifications and experience, taking into account the cost of living in Malaysia. Websites like Salary Explorer and JobStreet can provide insights into average salary ranges for various job roles in Malaysia.

Work Culture: Understanding the Malaysian Workplace

The work culture in Malaysia is generally professional and hierarchical. Respect for authority and seniority is important, and communication is often formal.

Here are some key aspects of the Malaysian work culture:

- **Punctuality:** Being on time for meetings and appointments is expected.

- **Dress Code:** The dress code in Malaysian workplaces varies depending on the industry and company culture. However, in general, professional attire is expected, particularly in corporate settings.

- **Communication Style:** Communication is often indirect and non-confrontational. Building relationships and trust is important in business dealings.

- **Meetings:** Meetings are usually structured and formal. Agendas are typically prepared in advance, and decisions are often made collectively.

- **Work-Life Balance:** Work-life balance is becoming increasingly important in Malaysia, particularly in multinational companies. However, long working hours are still common in some industries.

Business Opportunities: Entrepreneurship in Malaysia

Malaysia's business-friendly environment and government initiatives have fostered a thriving entrepreneurial ecosystem, attracting both local and foreign investors. If you're an expat with an entrepreneurial spirit, Malaysia offers a range of opportunities to set up and grow your business.

Government Incentives and Support

The Malaysian government has implemented several programs and incentives to encourage foreign investment and support entrepreneurship. These include:

- **Tax Incentives:** Tax breaks and exemptions are available for businesses in specific industries or those that meet certain criteria.

- **Grants and Funding:** Government grants and funding programs are available to support startups and small and medium enterprises (SMEs).

- **Special Economic Zones:** Special economic zones offer tax incentives, infrastructure support, and streamlined business registration processes.

- **Investment Promotion Agencies:** Government agencies like the Malaysian Investment Development Authority (MIDA) provide assistance to foreign investors, including guidance on business registration, incentives, and market opportunities.

Business Registration: Setting Up Your Company

The process of setting up a business in Malaysia is relatively straightforward, with clear guidelines and procedures. The Companies Commission of Malaysia (SSM) is the government agency responsible for business registration.

Here are the general steps involved:

1. **Company Name Reservation:** Reserve a unique name for your company with SSM.

2. **Company Incorporation:** Prepare and submit the necessary incorporation documents, including the company's constitution, details of directors and shareholders, and the registered office address.

3. **Business Licenses and Permits:** Depending on the nature of your business, you may need to obtain specific licenses and permits from relevant government agencies.

4. **Tax Registration:** Register for taxes with the Inland Revenue Board of Malaysia (IRB).

Choosing a Business Structure

There are several business structures to choose from in Malaysia, each with its own legal and tax implications:

- **Sole Proprietorship:** A simple structure for individuals operating a business under their own name.

- **Partnership:** A structure where two or more individuals agree to share profits and losses from a business.

- **Private Limited Company (Sdn Bhd):** A separate legal entity with limited liability for shareholders. This is the most common business structure for larger companies.

Networking and Resources: Connecting with the Business Community

Networking is crucial for entrepreneurial success in Malaysia. There are several organizations and resources to help you connect with the business community, including:

- **Chambers of Commerce:** Chambers of commerce, such as the Malaysian International Chamber of Commerce and Industry (MICCI), offer networking events, business support services, and advocacy for their members.

- **Business Associations:** Industry-specific business associations provide networking opportunities, industry insights, and support for businesses in their respective sectors.

- **Startup Incubators and Accelerators:** Incubators and accelerators provide mentorship, funding, and resources to support early-stage startups.

- **Networking Events:** Attend industry events, conferences, and workshops to connect with potential partners, investors, and customers.

Challenges and Considerations: Navigating the Business Landscape

While Malaysia offers a favorable environment for entrepreneurship, there are also challenges and considerations to be aware of:

- **Competition:** The Malaysian market is competitive, with both local and international companies vying for market share.

- **Cultural Nuances:** Understanding the cultural nuances and business etiquette in Malaysia is essential for successful business dealings.

- **Regulation and Compliance:** Malaysia has a relatively well-regulated business environment, with compliance requirements that need to be met. It's essential to stay informed about the latest regulations and seek professional advice when needed.

Making Your Mark: Thriving in the Malaysian Job Market

Whether you're seeking employment with a Malaysian company or embarking on an entrepreneurial journey, Malaysia's dynamic job market and business opportunities hold immense potential for expats. By understanding the in-demand industries, visa requirements, work culture, and the resources available to support entrepreneurship, you can position yourself for success and make a meaningful contribution to Malaysia's vibrant economy.

CHAPTER EIGHT: Setting Up Your Finances: Banking and Taxes

Moving to a new country necessitates setting up a new financial life. This is particularly important for expats who need to manage their finances across borders. Malaysia offers a robust and modern banking system, with a wide array of options to cater to the needs of both individuals and businesses. This chapter aims to equip you with the essential information about opening bank accounts, understanding the financial landscape, and navigating the tax system in Malaysia.

Banking in Malaysia: A World of Options

Malaysia boasts a sophisticated and well-regulated banking system, overseen by Bank Negara Malaysia (BNM), the central bank. You'll find a variety of banks, both local and international, offering a comprehensive range of financial services, from basic savings accounts and current accounts to credit cards, loans, and investment products.

Choosing the Right Bank

With numerous banks vying for your business, selecting the right one that aligns with your specific needs is crucial. Here are some factors to consider when choosing a bank in Malaysia:

- **Convenience and Accessibility:** Consider the bank's branch network and ATM availability, especially if you prefer in-person banking services. Major cities like Kuala Lumpur and Penang have a dense network of bank branches, while smaller towns may have limited options.

- **Online and Mobile Banking:** Most banks in Malaysia offer comprehensive online and mobile banking platforms, providing convenient access to your accounts and allowing you to manage your finances on the go.

- **International Banking Services:** If you frequently transfer money internationally or have financial commitments in your home country, look for banks with strong international banking capabilities.

- **Fees and Charges:** Banks have varying fee structures for account maintenance, ATM withdrawals, international transfers, and other services. Compare fees carefully to find a bank that offers competitive rates.

- **Customer Service:** Good customer service is crucial for a smooth banking experience. Read online reviews and ask for recommendations from other expats to gauge the bank's customer service reputation.

Opening a Bank Account: A Straightforward Process

Once you've chosen a bank, opening an account is generally a straightforward process. You'll need to provide the following documents:

- **Passport:** Your passport must be valid for at least six months beyond your intended stay in Malaysia.

- **Visa:** You'll need to present your valid visa, such as an Employment Pass, Dependent Pass, or MM2H visa.

- **Proof of Address:** This could be a tenancy agreement, utility bill, or a letter from your employer confirming your address in Malaysia.

- **Employment Letter (if applicable):** Some banks may require an employment letter from your employer in Malaysia.

The bank staff will guide you through the application process, which may involve filling out an application form and providing your signature specimens. Once your application is approved, you'll receive your account details, including your account number and ATM card.

Types of Bank Accounts

Malaysian banks offer various types of accounts to suit different needs:

- **Savings Account:** A basic account for saving money and earning interest.

- **Current Account:** An account for everyday transactions, such as receiving salary payments, paying bills, and making purchases.

- **Fixed Deposit Account:** An account for depositing a fixed amount of money for a specific period, earning a higher interest rate than savings accounts.

- **Foreign Currency Account:** An account for holding foreign currencies, which can be useful for expats who receive income in foreign currencies or need to make international payments.

Managing Your Finances: Key Tips for Expats

Here are some key tips for managing your finances effectively as an expat in Malaysia:

- **Budgeting:** Create a realistic budget that tracks your income and expenses, allowing you to monitor your spending and make informed financial decisions.

- **Currency Exchange:** Be mindful of exchange rates when converting currencies, as fluctuations can impact your finances. Consider using reputable money changers or online platforms for competitive exchange rates.

- **International Transfers:** If you need to send money overseas, compare transfer fees and exchange rates from different banks and money transfer services to find the most cost-effective option.

- **Credit Cards:** Credit cards can be convenient for purchases and emergencies, but use them responsibly and avoid accumulating high-interest debt.

- **Investments:** Explore investment options in Malaysia, such as unit trusts, mutual funds, or stocks, to grow your wealth. However, seek professional financial advice before making any investment decisions.

Understanding the Tax System

Malaysia has a territorial tax system, meaning that you are generally only taxed on income earned within the country. However, there are some exceptions and nuances that expats should be aware of.

Individual Income Tax

As an expat working in Malaysia, you are liable to pay individual income tax on your employment income. The tax year in Malaysia runs from January 1st to December 31st.

Tax rates for residents are progressive, ranging from 0% to 30%, depending on your income level. Non-residents are taxed at a flat rate of 30%.

Tax Exemptions and Deductions

The Malaysian tax system allows for various exemptions and deductions that can reduce your taxable income. Some common exemptions and deductions for expats include:

- **Personal Relief:** A basic exemption for all taxpayers.

- **Spouse Relief:** An exemption for married taxpayers.

- **Child Relief:** An exemption for each dependent child.

- **Education and Medical Expenses:** Deductions for certain education and medical expenses.

Filing Your Tax Return

You are required to file an annual income tax return with the IRB if you meet the minimum income threshold for tax residency. The deadline for filing your tax return is typically April 30th of the following year.

The IRB provides online filing facilities for taxpayers, making it convenient to submit your tax return electronically. You can also seek assistance from tax professionals or consult the IRB's website for guidance on tax filing procedures.

Goods and Services Tax (GST)

Malaysia replaced the previous Sales and Service Tax (SST) with a Goods and Services Tax (GST) of 6% in April 2015. However, after the change in government in 2018, the GST was abolished and replaced by the SST at a rate of 10% for sales and 6% for services, effective from September 2018.

Property Taxes

If you own property in Malaysia, you will be subject to property taxes, which are assessed by the local government authorities. Property taxes are based on the assessed value of your property and the prevailing tax rates in your area.

Seeking Professional Financial Advice

Navigating the financial landscape and tax system in a new country can be complex. It's advisable to seek professional financial advice from qualified accountants or tax consultants who are familiar with the Malaysian tax laws and regulations. They can help you optimize your tax liabilities, understand your financial obligations, and make informed financial decisions.

Setting up your finances and understanding the tax system are essential aspects of settling into your new life in Malaysia. By choosing the right bank, managing your money wisely, and staying informed about tax regulations, you can ensure a smooth financial transition and focus on enjoying the many opportunities that Malaysia has to offer.

CHAPTER NINE: Transportation: Getting Around Malaysia

Once you've settled into your new Malaysian home, you'll want to start exploring! And for that, you need to know how to get around. Luckily, Malaysia has a surprisingly diverse and comprehensive transportation system, from modern highways and efficient public transport to charming local buses and ferries. This chapter will guide you through the ins and outs of transportation in Malaysia, helping you navigate your way through cities, towns, and across the country.

Public Transportation: Your Ticket to Easy Travel

Malaysia's public transport system is generally efficient and affordable, making it a great option for both daily commutes and longer journeys. You'll find a variety of choices, each with its own strengths and quirks.

Trains: Connecting Cities and Towns

The train system in Malaysia is primarily operated by Keretapi Tanah Melayu (KTM), the national railway company. KTM offers a range of train services, connecting major cities and towns across Peninsular Malaysia, with a few lines extending into Thailand.

KTM Intercity: These trains provide long-distance services, connecting cities like Kuala Lumpur, Penang, Johor Bahru, and Singapore. They offer different classes of seating, from basic economy to more comfortable first-class options. Intercity trains can be a scenic and relaxing way to travel between cities, but journey times can be longer than by air or bus.

KTM Komuter: This commuter rail service operates within the Klang Valley (the metropolitan area surrounding Kuala Lumpur) and several other major cities, providing frequent and affordable transportation for daily commutes. Komuter trains are a popular choice for getting to work, school, and shopping malls within urban areas.

ETS (Electric Train Service): The ETS is a high-speed electric train service that operates on the West Coast Line, connecting Kuala Lumpur with major cities like Ipoh, Butterworth (for Penang), and Padang Besar (near the Thai border). ETS trains are significantly faster than regular KTM Intercity trains, offering a comfortable and efficient way to travel between cities.

KLIA Ekspres and KLIA Transit: These dedicated airport rail services connect Kuala Lumpur International Airport (KLIA) with KL Sentral, the main transportation hub in Kuala Lumpur. The KLIA Ekspres is a non-stop express service, while the KLIA Transit makes several stops along the way. Both services are fast, reliable, and offer a comfortable ride to and from the airport.

Buses: A Network That Reaches Every Corner

Buses are the most ubiquitous form of public transport in Malaysia, with an extensive network that reaches almost every corner of the country. You'll find a variety of bus operators, offering different types of services, from local city buses to long-distance express buses.

City Buses: Most major cities and towns in Malaysia have local bus services that operate on fixed routes, connecting different neighborhoods and commercial areas. City buses are generally affordable, but journey times can be unpredictable due to traffic congestion. You can pay for your fare on board using cash or a contactless card, but it's advisable to have the exact change ready.

Express Buses: Express buses offer long-distance services, connecting major cities and towns across Peninsular Malaysia and East Malaysia. They typically have comfortable seating, air conditioning, and sometimes even onboard toilets and entertainment systems. Express buses are often faster than trains, but they can be less comfortable for very long journeys.

Light Rail Transit (LRT) and Monorail: Navigating the Urban Jungle

Major cities like Kuala Lumpur and Penang have Light Rail Transit (LRT) systems that provide fast and efficient transportation within the city limits. LRT trains operate on elevated tracks, avoiding traffic congestion and offering quick journey times.

Kuala Lumpur also has a monorail line that runs through the heart of the city, connecting popular shopping malls, tourist attractions, and business districts.

Both LRT and monorail systems use contactless smart cards for payment. You can purchase these cards at train stations and top them up as needed.

Taxis: Convenient but Prone to Traffic

Taxis are readily available in most Malaysian cities and towns, offering convenient door-to-door transportation. However, taxis can be prone to traffic congestion, particularly in urban areas during peak hours.

Taxis in Malaysia are required by law to use meters, but it's always advisable to confirm that the meter is turned on before starting your journey. Some taxi drivers may attempt to negotiate a fixed fare, especially for longer journeys, but it's generally better to stick with the metered fare.

Ride-Hailing Services: Your Smartphone is Your Chauffeur

Ride-hailing services like Grab have revolutionized transportation in Malaysia, offering a convenient and often more affordable alternative to taxis. With the Grab app, you can easily book rides from your smartphone, track your driver's location, and pay electronically through the app.

Grab offers various ride options, from budget-friendly GrabCar rides to more comfortable GrabTaxi rides and even six-seater GrabCar Plus rides for larger groups.

Driving in Malaysia: Freedom to Explore at Your Own Pace

While public transportation in Malaysia is efficient, driving a car can offer a greater sense of freedom and flexibility to explore the country at your own pace. However, driving in Malaysia also comes with its own challenges, from navigating unfamiliar roads and traffic conditions to understanding local driving laws and regulations.

Obtaining a Driving License

If you're planning to drive in Malaysia, you'll need a valid driving license. Foreigners can drive in Malaysia using their home country driving license for up to three months. However, for longer stays, you'll need to convert your foreign license to a Malaysian driving license.

The process for converting a foreign driving license involves:

1. **Visit a JPJ (Road Transport Department) office:** Locate the nearest JPJ office and submit your application for a Malaysian driving license conversion.

2. **Required Documents:** You'll need to present your original foreign driving license, a certified translation of your license (if it's not in English), your passport, visa, and other supporting documents.

3. **Fees:** There is a fee for the license conversion process.

4. **Processing Time:** The processing time can vary, but typically takes a few days to a couple of weeks.

5. **Driving Test (if required):** Depending on your nationality and the type of driving license you hold, you may be required to take a written or practical driving test.

Understanding Traffic Rules and Regulations

Traffic laws in Malaysia are generally similar to those in other countries, but there are some key differences to be aware of:

- **Driving on the Left:** Cars in Malaysia drive on the left-hand side of the road.

- **Seat Belts:** Wearing seat belts is mandatory for both drivers and passengers.

- **Mobile Phone Use:** Using a mobile phone while driving is strictly prohibited. Hands-free devices are allowed.

- **Drinking and Driving:** Driving under the influence of alcohol is a serious offense in Malaysia, with strict penalties enforced.

- **Speed Limits:** Speed limits vary depending on the type of road and location. Pay attention to speed limit signs and adhere to them.

- **Toll Roads:** Many highways in Malaysia are toll roads. Electronic toll collection systems are in place, so ensure you have a Touch 'n Go card or SmartTAG device in your vehicle.

Road Conditions and Traffic Congestion

Road conditions in Malaysia vary. Highways are generally well-maintained, but some rural roads can be narrow, winding, and poorly lit.

Traffic congestion can be a significant issue in major cities like Kuala Lumpur, particularly during peak hours. Plan your journeys accordingly, allowing extra time for travel during rush hour.

Parking: Finding a Spot in Busy Areas

Parking can be a challenge in busy urban areas. Look for designated parking lots or street parking, but be sure to pay attention to parking restrictions and display a valid parking coupon or use a parking app if required.

Other Modes of Transportation: Boats, Planes, and More

Beyond the primary modes of transportation, Malaysia offers a variety of other ways to get around:

Ferries: Island Hopping and Coastal Connections

Ferries provide connections to various islands and coastal towns in Malaysia. They are a popular way to travel to Langkawi, Penang, Tioman Island, and other island destinations.

Ferry services vary in terms of frequency, comfort, and journey times. Check schedules and book tickets in advance, especially during peak season.

Domestic Flights: Connecting East and West Malaysia

Domestic flights connect Peninsular Malaysia with East Malaysia (Sabah and Sarawak), as well as between major cities and islands. Airlines like Malaysia Airlines, AirAsia, and Malindo Air offer domestic flights, providing a convenient and relatively affordable way to travel long distances.

Motorcycle Taxis (Motosikal): A Quick Way Through Traffic

In some urban areas, motorcycle taxis, locally known as "motosikal", offer a quick and nimble way to weave through traffic congestion. However, motorcycle taxis can be less safe than other modes of transportation, and it's advisable to wear a helmet and exercise caution.

Trishaws (Becak): A Charming Way to Explore Heritage Areas

Trishaws, or "becak", are three-wheeled pedal-powered vehicles commonly found in heritage areas and tourist spots. They offer a charming and leisurely way to explore historic neighborhoods. Negotiate the fare with the driver before starting your journey.

Getting Around: Your Transportation Toolkit

Here are some additional tips to help you navigate your way around Malaysia:

- **Plan Your Journeys in Advance:** Use online mapping services like Google Maps or Waze to plan your routes and check traffic conditions.

- **Download Transportation Apps:** Apps like Grab, MyRapid (for KL's public transport system), and Moovit can be helpful for booking rides, checking schedules, and finding the best routes.

- **Learn Some Basic Malay Phrases:** Knowing a few basic Malay phrases related to transportation can be helpful, especially when interacting with local drivers or asking for directions.

- **Stay Informed About Local News and Updates:** Keep an eye on local news and traffic updates to stay informed about any road closures, accidents, or other disruptions that might affect your travel plans.

- **Be Mindful of Safety:** Exercise caution when traveling, particularly at night or in unfamiliar areas. Keep your belongings secure and avoid walking alone in poorly lit or isolated areas.

Exploring Malaysia's diverse landscapes, vibrant cities, and charming towns is a rewarding experience. By understanding the various transportation options available, planning your journeys in advance, and embracing the local quirks and customs, you can navigate your way through the country with ease and make the most of your Malaysian adventure.

CHAPTER TEN: Language: Communicating in a Multilingual Society

Moving to Malaysia means immersing yourself in a vibrant tapestry of languages. While Bahasa Malaysia, the national language, serves as the lingua franca, you'll encounter a fascinating blend of dialects, languages, and accents that reflect the country's rich multicultural heritage. This chapter will guide you through the linguistic landscape of Malaysia, providing insights into the key languages spoken, the role of English, tips for effective communication, and resources for language learning.

Bahasa Malaysia: The Language of Unity

Bahasa Malaysia, also known as Malay, is the official language of Malaysia, spoken by the majority of the population. It serves as the language of government, education, and everyday communication, uniting the diverse ethnic groups that call Malaysia home.

For expats planning to live and work in Malaysia, learning at least some basic Bahasa Malaysia is highly beneficial. It will not only enhance your daily interactions but also demonstrate your respect for the local culture and facilitate deeper connections with Malaysians.

English: A Widely Spoken Second Language

English holds a prominent position in Malaysia as a widely spoken second language. It's the language of business, commerce, and higher education, and you'll find it commonly used in urban areas, shopping malls, restaurants, and tourist destinations.

Many Malaysians are fluent in English, particularly those in professional fields and the younger generation. This makes it relatively easy for expats to communicate and navigate daily life in Malaysia. However, venturing into rural areas or interacting with older generations may require some basic Bahasa Malaysia skills.

Manglish: A Uniquely Malaysian Blend

Manglish is a colloquial form of English spoken in Malaysia, incorporating elements of Bahasa Malaysia, Chinese dialects, and Tamil. It's a dynamic and evolving language, reflecting the country's multicultural influences. While Manglish is widely understood among Malaysians, it can sometimes be challenging for expats to decipher, especially in its more informal forms.

Chinese Dialects: A Reflection of Heritage

Chinese Malaysians constitute a significant portion of the population, and they speak a variety of Chinese dialects, including Mandarin, Cantonese, Hokkien, Hakka, Teochew, and Hainanese. The most common dialects spoken vary by region, with Cantonese being more prevalent in Kuala Lumpur and Hokkien in Penang.

While Mandarin is the official language of China and is promoted in schools, many Chinese Malaysians continue to use their respective dialects in daily communication within their communities.

Tamil: The Language of the Indian Community

The Indian community in Malaysia primarily speaks Tamil, although other South Indian languages, such as Telugu and Malayalam, are also spoken to a lesser extent. Tamil is used in daily communication within the Indian community, as well as in some schools and temples.

Indigenous Languages: A Linguistic Tapestry

The indigenous communities in both Peninsular Malaysia and East Malaysia have their own unique languages and dialects, adding to the linguistic diversity of the country. While some indigenous languages are spoken by large communities, others are endangered, with only a few remaining speakers.

Tips for Effective Communication: Bridging the Language Gaps

Communicating effectively in a multilingual society like Malaysia involves a combination of language skills, cultural sensitivity, and patience. Here are some tips to enhance your communication experience:

- **Learn Some Basic Bahasa Malaysia:** Even a few basic phrases, such as greetings, simple questions, and numbers, can go a long way in showing respect and facilitating daily interactions.

- **Speak Slowly and Clearly:** When speaking English, enunciate clearly and avoid using slang or idioms that may not be universally understood.

- **Be Patient and Understanding:** Not everyone you encounter will be fluent in English. Be patient with those who may struggle to communicate and try to find alternative ways to convey your message, such as using gestures or simple drawings.

- **Use Translation Apps or Dictionaries:** Smartphone translation apps and online dictionaries can be handy tools for bridging language gaps and understanding unfamiliar words or phrases.

- **Observe Body Language and Nonverbal Cues:** Pay attention to body language and nonverbal cues, as these can often convey meaning even when words fail.

- **Ask for Clarification:** Don't be afraid to ask for clarification if you don't understand something. Most Malaysians are happy to help and will appreciate your effort to communicate.

- **Embrace the Linguistic Diversity:** Be open to learning about the different languages and dialects spoken in

Malaysia. It's a fascinating journey of linguistic discovery that will enrich your cultural experience.

Language Learning Resources: Unlocking the Doors to Communication

If you're keen on learning Bahasa Malaysia or other languages spoken in Malaysia, there are numerous resources available to support your language journey:

- **Language Schools:** Several language schools in Malaysia offer Bahasa Malaysia courses for foreigners, ranging from beginner to advanced levels.

- **Online Language Learning Platforms:** Websites and apps like Duolingo, Babbel, and Rosetta Stone provide interactive language courses that you can access anytime, anywhere.

- **Language Exchange Partners:** Connect with Malaysians who are interested in learning your native language and practice speaking Bahasa Malaysia with them in a language exchange partnership.

- **Books and Language Learning Materials:** Bookstores and online retailers offer a variety of textbooks, dictionaries, and language learning materials to support your studies.

- **Immersion:** One of the best ways to learn a language is through immersion. Surround yourself with the language by watching local TV shows, listening to Malaysian music, and engaging in conversations with Malaysians whenever possible.

Embracing the Multilingual Tapestry: A Key to Cultural Connection

Navigating the linguistic landscape of Malaysia is an integral part of the expat experience. By embracing the country's multilingual heritage, learning some basic Bahasa Malaysia, and utilizing language learning resources, you can unlock the doors to effective communication, build deeper connections with the local community, and gain a greater appreciation for the richness and diversity of Malaysian culture.

CHAPTER ELEVEN: Malaysian Culture: Customs and Etiquette

As you prepare for your move to Malaysia, understanding the local culture and social etiquette is key to a smooth transition and a rewarding experience. Malaysian society is a fascinating blend of traditions, values, and customs, influenced by its diverse ethnic groups, predominantly Malay, Chinese, and Indian, each with its unique cultural heritage. This chapter will delve into the key aspects of Malaysian culture and provide practical tips on navigating social interactions, respecting local customs, and embracing the warmth and hospitality of the Malaysian people.

A Multicultural Mosaic: Respecting Diversity

Malaysia's multiculturalism is one of its most defining features, a vibrant tapestry woven from the traditions, values, and customs of its diverse ethnic groups. While Malay culture forms the foundation of Malaysian society, Chinese, Indian, and indigenous influences add rich layers to this cultural mosaic.

One of the first things you'll notice in Malaysia is the harmonious coexistence of different religions, languages, cuisines, and traditions. Temples, mosques, and churches stand side by side, a testament to the country's religious tolerance and harmony. Festivals celebrated by different ethnic groups are often enjoyed by all Malaysians, creating a shared sense of cultural identity.

As an expat, it's crucial to approach this cultural diversity with respect and sensitivity. Take the time to learn about the customs and traditions of the different ethnic groups, appreciate their unique perspectives, and avoid making generalizations or assumptions. Embrace the opportunity to broaden your horizons and experience the richness of Malaysian culture in all its forms.

Social Etiquette: Navigating Interactions with Grace

Understanding and adhering to local social etiquette is essential for building positive relationships and showing respect for Malaysian culture. Here are some key aspects of Malaysian social etiquette:

Greetings: A Warm and Respectful Start

Greetings in Malaysia are generally warm and respectful. The most common greeting is "Selamat pagi" (good morning), "Selamat tengah hari" (good afternoon), or "Selamat petang" (good evening), depending on the time of day.

When greeting someone older or of higher status, it's customary to use the honorific title "Encik" (Mr.), "Puan" (Mrs.), or "Cik" (Miss) before their name. For those with professional titles, such as "Doctor" or "Professor," it's respectful to address them by their title.

Handshakes are common between men, while women may greet each other with a nod or a slight bow. Among Malays, a more traditional greeting involves placing your right hand over your heart as a sign of respect.

Communication Style: Indirect and Non-Confrontational

Malaysian communication style tends to be indirect and non-confrontational. Directness and assertiveness, while common in some Western cultures, may be perceived as rude or aggressive in Malaysia. It's important to be mindful of tone of voice and body language, as these can convey subtle meanings.

When expressing opinions or disagreements, it's best to do so politely and diplomatically, avoiding any language that could be interpreted as confrontational. Malaysians value harmony and face-saving, so it's crucial to maintain a respectful and considerate approach in communication.

Body Language: Respectful Gestures and Nonverbal Cues

Body language plays an important role in Malaysian communication. Here are some nonverbal cues to be aware of:

- **Eye Contact:** Maintaining moderate eye contact is generally considered respectful, but prolonged staring can be seen as rude or aggressive.

- **Smiling:** Smiling is a common and welcoming gesture in Malaysia, conveying friendliness and approachability.

- **Pointing:** Pointing with the index finger is considered rude. Instead, use your right hand with your fingers together to gesture or indicate direction.

- **Feet:** Showing the soles of your feet or pointing your feet at someone is considered disrespectful.

- **Head:** The head is considered sacred in Malay culture. Avoid touching someone's head, even children's.

Dress Code: Modesty and Respect

Malaysian society generally values modesty in dress. While casual attire is acceptable in most settings, it's advisable to avoid revealing clothing, particularly when visiting religious sites or attending formal events.

When visiting mosques, women are expected to cover their heads with a scarf or shawl, and both men and women should dress modestly, covering their shoulders and knees.

Dining Etiquette: Sharing Meals and Showing Appreciation

Dining is an important social activity in Malaysia, and there are certain customs and etiquette to follow:

- **Wait to be Seated:** If you're invited to a dinner party or formal event, wait to be seated by the host.

- **Use Your Right Hand:** In Malay culture, the right hand is considered clean and is used for eating, shaking hands, and giving or receiving items. Avoid using your left hand for these actions.

- **Sharing is Caring:** Malaysian meals often involve sharing dishes. Take small portions from the shared dishes and avoid taking more than your fair share.

- **Finishing Your Plate:** It's considered polite to finish the food on your plate, showing appreciation for the meal.

- **Saying "Thank You":** Express your gratitude to the host for the meal by saying "Terima kasih" (thank you).

Gift-Giving: A Token of Appreciation

Gift-giving is a common practice in Malaysia, expressing gratitude, strengthening relationships, or marking special occasions. Here are some tips for gift-giving:

- **Wrap Gifts:** Wrap gifts neatly and presentably.

- **Give and Receive with Both Hands:** Use both hands when giving or receiving a gift.

- **Don't Open Gifts Immediately:** It's generally considered polite to open gifts later, in private, unless the giver insists you open it immediately.

- **Avoid Certain Gifts:** Gifts containing alcohol or pork products should be avoided, particularly when giving gifts to Muslims.

Visiting a Home: Respectful Customs

If you're invited to a Malaysian home, here are some customs to observe:

- **Remove Your Shoes:** It's customary to remove your shoes before entering a home.

- **Bring a Small Gift:** Bringing a small gift, such as fruits, sweets, or flowers, is a thoughtful gesture.

- **Accept Refreshments:** It's polite to accept refreshments offered by the host, even if you're not thirsty or hungry.

- **Engage in Conversation:** Show interest in the host and their family by engaging in conversation. Ask questions about their culture, traditions, or interests.

Religious Sensitivity: Understanding and Respecting Beliefs

As a multicultural and multi-religious society, Malaysia places great importance on religious harmony and respect. While Islam is the official religion, the country embraces a diverse range of faiths, including Buddhism, Christianity, Hinduism, Sikhism, and Taoism.

Here are some key points to remember:

- **Dress Modestly When Visiting Religious Sites:** When visiting mosques, temples, churches, or other religious sites, dress modestly and respectfully. Women may be required to cover their heads or shoulders.

- **Be Mindful of Religious Practices:** Be aware of the religious practices and customs of different faiths and avoid engaging in behaviors that may be considered offensive or disrespectful.

- **Avoid Discussing Religion:** Unless you are well-acquainted with someone, it's generally best to avoid discussing religion, as it can be a sensitive topic.

Embracing Malaysian Culture: Tips for a Rewarding Experience

Here are some additional tips to help you embrace Malaysian culture and enjoy a rewarding experience:

- **Be Open-Minded and Curious:** Approach Malaysian culture with an open mind and a genuine curiosity to learn and understand different perspectives.

- **Ask Questions:** Don't be afraid to ask questions about local customs or traditions. Malaysians are generally friendly and happy to share their culture with foreigners.

- **Attend Cultural Events:** Participate in cultural events, such as festivals, performances, or exhibitions, to immerse yourself in the richness of Malaysian culture.

- **Try Local Cuisine:** Malaysian cuisine is a delicious reflection of the country's multicultural heritage. Venture beyond familiar dishes and try local delicacies to savor the flavors of Malaysia.

- **Learn Some Basic Bahasa Malaysia:** Learning a few basic Malay phrases can enhance your daily interactions and show your respect for the local culture.

- **Make Local Friends:** Connecting with Malaysians can provide valuable insights into the culture, customs, and way of life. Be open to forming friendships with people from different backgrounds.

Moving to Malaysia opens doors to a fascinating cultural journey. By embracing the country's multiculturalism, understanding social etiquette, respecting religious sensitivities, and approaching the local culture with an open mind, you can create a positive and enriching experience for yourself and build meaningful connections with the warm and hospitable Malaysian people.

CHAPTER TWELVE: Religion and Religious Harmony in Malaysia

Religion plays a significant role in the lives of many Malaysians, shaping their values, customs, and social interactions. As you embark on your journey as an expat in Malaysia, understanding the country's religious landscape and the principles of religious harmony that underpin its society is essential for fostering respectful relationships and navigating cultural nuances. This chapter will provide insights into the major religions practiced in Malaysia, the concept of religious freedom enshrined in the Constitution, and the ways in which religious harmony is fostered and maintained in this diverse nation.

Islam: The Official Religion and Its Influence

Islam holds a prominent place in Malaysia, being the official religion of the Federation. The majority of Malays are Muslims, and Islamic principles and practices are deeply intertwined with Malay culture and traditions. Mosques dot the landscape, the call to prayer echoes five times a day, and Islamic holidays are observed as national holidays.

The influence of Islam extends beyond religious practices, shaping social norms, values, and even aspects of governance. Islamic principles are reflected in the legal system, particularly in matters concerning family law and inheritance for Muslims. However, it's important to note that Malaysia is not an Islamic state, and the Constitution guarantees freedom of religion for all citizens.

Religious Freedom: A Cornerstone of Malaysian Society

The Malaysian Constitution enshrines the principle of religious freedom, allowing citizens to practice their chosen faith without interference or discrimination. This commitment to religious liberty is a testament to the country's multicultural heritage and the harmonious coexistence of different faiths.

While Islam holds a special status as the official religion, other religions are freely practiced and respected. Buddhists, Christians, Hindus, Sikhs, Taoists, and followers of other faiths are free to worship, build places of worship, and observe their religious holidays.

The government plays a role in fostering interfaith dialogue and understanding, promoting tolerance and respect among different religious communities. Interfaith councils and organizations work towards building bridges between faiths, addressing common concerns, and promoting peace and harmony.

Buddhism: A Prominent Faith with Deep Roots

Buddhism has deep roots in Malaysia, particularly among the Chinese community. Buddhist temples, with their ornate architecture and serene atmosphere, are common sights throughout the country. The teachings of Buddha emphasize compassion, wisdom, and the pursuit of enlightenment.

Wesak Day, which commemorates the birth, enlightenment, and death of Buddha, is a national holiday in Malaysia, celebrated with processions, offerings, and acts of charity.

Christianity: A Diverse and Growing Faith

Christianity is another prominent religion in Malaysia, practiced by a diverse community comprising various denominations, including Catholicism, Protestantism, and other Christian groups. Churches are found throughout the country, and Christian holidays, such as Christmas and Easter, are widely celebrated.

Christianity is particularly prevalent in East Malaysia (Sabah and Sarawak), where a significant portion of the indigenous population has embraced the faith.

Hinduism: A Vibrant Faith with Colorful Traditions

Hinduism is a vibrant and colorful faith, brought to Malaysia by Indian immigrants centuries ago. Hindu temples, adorned with intricate carvings and statues of deities, are centers of religious and cultural life for the Indian community.

Deepavali, the Festival of Lights, is a major Hindu holiday celebrated in Malaysia with great enthusiasm. Homes are decorated with colorful lights, families gather for prayers and feasts, and fireworks illuminate the night sky. Thaipusam, another important Hindu festival, involves a procession of devotees carrying kavadis (ornate structures) as an act of penance and devotion to Lord Murugan.

Other Faiths: Adding to the Religious Tapestry

Besides the major religions, Malaysia is home to followers of other faiths, including Sikhism, Taoism, and indigenous beliefs. Gurdwaras, Sikh temples, serve as places of worship and community gathering for the Sikh community. Taoist temples, with their distinctive architecture and emphasis on balance and harmony, are also found throughout the country.

The indigenous communities in Malaysia often practice animistic beliefs, revering nature spirits and ancestral deities. Their traditions and rituals are deeply connected to the land and their cultural heritage.

Religious Harmony: A Shared Value and a Lived Reality

Religious harmony is not merely a constitutional principle in Malaysia but a lived reality. Malaysians from different faiths often interact and celebrate each other's festivals, fostering a spirit of mutual respect and understanding.

Interfaith dialogues, community events, and educational initiatives promote tolerance and appreciation for different beliefs. Schools often organize visits to places of worship of various faiths, allowing students to learn about different religions and foster interfaith understanding from a young age.

The government actively promotes religious harmony through various initiatives, including:

- **Interfaith Councils:** Interfaith councils, comprising representatives from different religious communities, provide a platform for dialogue, cooperation, and addressing common concerns.

- **Harmony Week:** The annual Harmony Week celebrations showcase the diversity of faiths in Malaysia and promote interfaith understanding through cultural performances, exhibitions, and community events.

- **Religious Education:** Religious education is incorporated into the school curriculum, providing students with a basic understanding of different religions and promoting tolerance and respect.

Navigating Religious Sensitivities: Tips for Expats

As an expat in Malaysia, respecting religious sensitivities is paramount for building positive relationships and integrating into the community. Here are some practical tips:

- **Dress Modestly:** When visiting religious sites or attending religious events, dress modestly and respectfully. Avoid revealing clothing, particularly when entering mosques or temples. Women may be required to cover their heads with a scarf or shawl.

- **Be Mindful of Religious Practices:** Be aware of the religious practices and customs of different faiths and avoid engaging in behaviors that may be considered offensive or disrespectful. For example, during the month of Ramadan, when Muslims fast from dawn to dusk, it's respectful to refrain from eating or drinking in public during fasting hours.

- **Avoid Sensitive Topics:** Unless you are well-acquainted with someone, it's generally best to avoid discussing religion or making comments that could be interpreted as insensitive or disrespectful.

- **Ask for Guidance:** If you are unsure about any religious customs or practices, don't hesitate to ask for guidance from your Malaysian friends or colleagues. Most Malaysians are happy to share their knowledge and help you navigate cultural nuances.

Embracing the Spirit of Harmony: A Rewarding Journey

Malaysia's religious landscape is a testament to the country's multicultural heritage and the enduring principles of religious freedom and harmony that underpin its society. As you embark on your expat journey, embrace the opportunity to learn about different faiths, appreciate the spirit of tolerance and respect, and contribute to the harmonious tapestry of Malaysian life.

CHAPTER THIRTEEN: Food: A Culinary Journey Through Malaysia's Diverse Flavors

Prepare to embark on a gastronomic adventure, because moving to Malaysia is a culinary journey like no other. This country is a true food lover's paradise, boasting a mind-boggling array of flavors, aromas, and culinary traditions that reflect its rich multicultural heritage. From spicy Malay curries and fragrant Chinese stir-fries to flavorful Indian dishes and unique indigenous delicacies, Malaysia's food scene is a symphony of tastes and textures that will tantalize your taste buds and leave you craving for more.

This chapter will serve as your guide to navigating the culinary delights of Malaysia, exploring the key influences that have shaped its cuisine, the must-try dishes that define its culinary identity, the best places to experience this gastronomic adventure, and essential tips for navigating the local food scene.

A Fusion of Flavors: The Story Behind Malaysian Cuisine

Malaysian cuisine is a fascinating fusion of Malay, Chinese, Indian, and indigenous influences, a reflection of the country's history as a melting pot of cultures. Centuries of trade, migration, and cultural exchange have resulted in a culinary tapestry that is both diverse and harmonious.

Malay Cuisine: The Foundation of Flavor

Malay cuisine forms the foundation of Malaysian food, characterized by its bold flavors, aromatic spices, and generous use of coconut milk, chilies, and herbs. Rice is a staple, often served with an assortment of side dishes, such as curries, stir-fries, and sambals (spicy chili pastes).

Key ingredients in Malay cuisine include:

- **Coconut Milk:** Lending a rich, creamy texture and a subtle sweetness to curries, soups, and desserts.

- **Chilies:** Adding fiery heat and depth of flavor to a wide range of dishes.

- **Lemongrass:** Infusing dishes with a distinctive citrusy aroma and flavor.

- **Galangal:** A ginger-like root, imparting a warm, earthy flavor to curries and soups.

- **Turmeric:** Adding a vibrant yellow color and a warm, earthy flavor to curries and rice dishes.

- **Shrimp Paste (Belacan):** A pungent fermented shrimp paste, adding a unique umami flavor to sambals, dips, and stir-fries.

Chinese Influence: From Noodles to Stir-Fries

Chinese immigrants have left an indelible mark on Malaysian cuisine, introducing a wide array of dishes, cooking techniques, and ingredients. Noodles, stir-fries, dumplings, and roasted meats are staples of Chinese-influenced Malaysian food.

Key elements of Chinese influence include:

- **Soy Sauce:** A salty, savory condiment used extensively in marinades, stir-fries, and dipping sauces.

- **Oyster Sauce:** A thick, savory sauce made from oyster extracts, adding a rich umami flavor to stir-fries and noodles.

- **Noodles:** From thin rice noodles to thick wheat noodles, noodles are a versatile ingredient used in soups, stir-fries, and salads.

- **Stir-Frying:** A high-heat cooking technique that results in flavorful and crispy dishes.

- **Dim Sum:** Bite-sized portions of steamed or fried dumplings, buns, and other savory treats, often enjoyed as a brunch or light meal.

Indian Flavors: Spice and Aromatic Delights

Indian cuisine, with its aromatic spices, rich curries, and flavorful breads, has also significantly influenced Malaysian food. Indian-inspired dishes are characterized by their complex flavors, often combining a blend of spices like cumin, coriander, turmeric, and chili powder.

Key elements of Indian influence include:

- **Curries:** Aromatic and flavorful stews, often made with coconut milk, yogurt, or tomato-based sauces.

- **Tandoori:** A cooking technique where meats or vegetables are marinated in yogurt and spices and cooked in a tandoor (clay oven), resulting in a smoky flavor and tender texture.

- **Naan:** A soft, leavened flatbread, often served with curries or as a wrap for kebabs.

- **Biryani:** A mixed rice dish, layered with meat, vegetables, and aromatic spices.

Indigenous Cuisine: A Taste of Tradition

The indigenous communities in Malaysia have their own unique culinary traditions, often utilizing ingredients sourced from the surrounding forests and rivers. These dishes, passed down through generations, offer a glimpse into the cultural heritage of these communities.

Indigenous cuisines vary depending on the region and ethnic group but often include:

- **Wild Plants and Herbs:** Indigenous communities have a deep knowledge of local flora, incorporating wild plants and herbs into their dishes for flavor and medicinal purposes.

- **Game Meats:** Hunting is a traditional practice in some indigenous communities, and game meats, such as wild boar or deer, may be incorporated into their dishes.

- **Fermented Foods:** Fermentation is a common technique used to preserve food and enhance flavor. Indigenous cuisines may include fermented ingredients like tempoyak (fermented durian) or budu (fermented anchovies).

Must-Try Dishes: A Culinary Bucket List for Your Malaysian Adventure

Prepare your taste buds for a culinary adventure, because Malaysia's food scene is a symphony of flavors and textures that will leave you craving for more. Here's a bucket list of must-try dishes that define the country's culinary identity:

Nasi Lemak: The National Dish of Malaysia

Nasi lemak, meaning "rich rice" in Malay, is considered the national dish of Malaysia, a beloved breakfast staple enjoyed throughout the day. It typically consists of fragrant coconut rice steamed with pandan leaves, served with a variety of accompaniments, including:

- **Sambal:** A spicy chili paste, often made with shrimp paste (belacan), chilies, onions, and garlic.

- **Fried Anchovies (Ikan Bilis):** Tiny, crispy fried anchovies, adding a salty and savory crunch.

- **Peanuts:** Roasted peanuts, providing a nutty flavor and textural contrast.

- **Cucumber Slices:** Adding a refreshing crunch and coolness.

- **Hard-Boiled Egg:** A protein-rich addition.

Nasi lemak is often served wrapped in banana leaves, adding a subtle aroma to the rice. It can be enjoyed on its own or with various additions, such as fried chicken (ayam goreng), beef rendang (spicy dry curry), or sambal sotong (spicy squid).

Laksa: A Spicy Noodle Soup Symphony

Laksa is a popular spicy noodle soup dish, found in various regional variations throughout Malaysia. The key element of laksa is the rich and flavorful broth, which can be based on coconut milk, tamarind, or fish stock, often spiced with a blend of chilies, lemongrass, galangal, and other aromatics.

Some popular variations of laksa include:

- **Curry Laksa:** A coconut milk-based broth, rich and creamy, often flavored with curry powder, lemongrass, and galangal. It's typically served with thick rice noodles, chicken, prawns, tofu puffs, and bean sprouts, garnished with fresh herbs.

- **Asam Laksa:** A tangy and spicy tamarind-based broth, often flavored with fish, lemongrass, galangal, and chilies. It's typically served with thin rice noodles, shredded fish, pineapple, cucumber, onions, and mint.

Roti Canai: The Versatile Flatbread Delight

Roti canai is a beloved Malaysian flatbread, a staple at breakfast stalls, mamak (Indian Muslim) restaurants, and hawker centers. It's made from a simple dough of flour, water, and ghee (clarified butter), which is repeatedly stretched, flipped, and folded to create thin, flaky layers. The dough is then cooked on a flat griddle until golden brown and crispy.

Roti canai can be enjoyed on its own or dipped into a variety of curries, such as dhal (lentil curry), chicken curry, or fish curry. It's also often served with a side of sambal and a sprinkle of sugar.

Satay: Skewered and Grilled to Perfection

Satay is a popular street food dish in Malaysia, consisting of skewered and grilled meats, typically chicken, beef, or mutton. The meats are marinated in a blend of spices, including turmeric, lemongrass, and cumin, then grilled over charcoal until tender and slightly charred.

Satay is often served with a peanut dipping sauce, made with ground roasted peanuts, chilies, onions, and tamarind. It's a perfect snack or light meal, enjoyed with a side of ketupat (compressed rice cakes) or nasi impit (compressed rice).

Rendang: A Spicy Dry Curry to Savor

Rendang is a rich and flavorful dry curry dish, originating from Indonesia but widely enjoyed in Malaysia. It's typically made with beef, chicken, or mutton, slow-cooked in coconut milk and a blend of spices, including lemongrass, galangal, chilies, and turmeric. The dish is simmered for hours until the meat is incredibly tender and the sauce has reduced to a thick, flavorful paste.

Rendang can be enjoyed with rice, ketupat, or roti canai. It's a dish best savored slowly, allowing the complex flavors to develop on your palate.

Char Kway Teow: A Stir-Fried Noodle Sensation

Char kway teow is a popular stir-fried noodle dish, a staple at hawker centers and Chinese restaurants in Malaysia. It's made with flat rice noodles, stir-fried with a combination of ingredients, including:

- **Soy Sauce:** Adding a salty and savory flavor.

- **Sweet Soy Sauce:** Providing a touch of sweetness and a deeper color.

- **Oyster Sauce:** Lending a rich umami flavor.

- **Fish Cake:** Adding a chewy texture and a hint of seafood flavor.

- **Chinese Sausage:** Providing a smoky and savory flavor.

- **Bean Sprouts:** Adding a crunchy texture.

- **Chives:** Infusing a fresh oniony flavor.

The dish is cooked over high heat, ensuring the noodles are slightly charred and the flavors are intense.

Nasi Kandar: A Rice Dish with a Symphony of Flavors

Nasi kandar is a popular rice dish originating from Penang, where Indian Muslim traders, known as "Mamak," have left a unique culinary mark. It's a dish that embodies the essence of Malaysian fusion cuisine, with a base of steamed rice served with a variety of curries, gravies, and side dishes, including:

- **Chicken Curry:** Aromatic and flavorful, often made with coconut milk and spices.

- **Fish Curry:** Tangy and spicy, typically made with tamarind and chilies.

- **Beef Rendang:** Rich and flavorful dry curry, slow-cooked in coconut milk and spices.

- **Fried Chicken:** Crispy and juicy, often marinated in spices before frying.

- **Sambal:** A spicy chili paste, adding fiery heat to the dish.

- **Vegetables:** A variety of vegetables, such as okra, eggplant, and cabbage, often cooked in curries or stir-fried.

Mee Goreng: A Spicy Fried Noodle Delight

Mee goreng, meaning "fried noodles" in Malay, is a popular street food dish found throughout Malaysia. It's made with yellow noodles (egg noodles), stir-fried with a combination of ingredients, including:

- **Soy Sauce:** Adding a salty and savory flavor.

- **Sweet Soy Sauce:** Providing a touch of sweetness.

- **Chili Paste:** Adding a fiery kick.

- **Vegetables:** A variety of vegetables, such as cabbage, bean sprouts, and carrots, adding texture and flavor.

- **Protein:** Often includes chicken, beef, prawns, or tofu.

The noodles are stir-fried over high heat, ensuring they are slightly charred and the flavors are intense. Mee goreng is often garnished with a fried egg and a sprinkle of fried shallots.

Experiencing the Culinary Adventure: Where to Eat in Malaysia

From bustling hawker centers and street food stalls to cozy cafes and fine dining restaurants, Malaysia offers a diverse range of culinary experiences to satisfy every taste and budget. Here's a glimpse into the best places to savor the flavors of Malaysia:

Hawker Centers and Food Courts: A Feast for the Senses

Hawker centers and food courts are the heart and soul of Malaysia's food scene, offering a mind-boggling array of dishes, from local favorites to international cuisines, all under one roof. These bustling food havens are a feast for the senses, with aromas wafting through the air, sizzling woks in action, and a cacophony of chatter and laughter.

Here's why you should experience hawker centers and food courts:

- **Variety and Choice:** You'll find a wide selection of food stalls, each specializing in a particular dish or cuisine, offering a chance to sample a variety of flavors.

- **Affordability:** Hawker centers and food courts are renowned for their affordability, making them a budget-friendly option for enjoying delicious meals.

- **Authenticity:** The food stalls are often run by families who have been perfecting their recipes for generations, offering a taste of authentic Malaysian flavors.

- **Social Atmosphere:** Hawker centers are social hubs, where people from all walks of life gather to eat, chat, and enjoy the lively atmosphere.

Mamak Restaurants: A Unique Malaysian Experience

Mamak restaurants, run by Indian Muslims, are a unique Malaysian institution, serving a fusion of Indian, Malay, and Chinese dishes. These open-air restaurants are often open 24 hours a day, making them a popular spot for late-night meals or a casual hangout with friends.

Mamak restaurants are known for their:

- **Roti Canai:** The ubiquitous Malaysian flatbread, served with a variety of curries and dips.

- **Teh Tarik:** "Pulled tea," a frothy milk tea made by repeatedly pouring the tea between two containers, creating a creamy texture.

- **Maggi Goreng:** A popular dish of instant noodles stir-fried with vegetables, meat, and spices.

- **Nasi Kandar:** A rice dish with a variety of curries, gravies, and side dishes.

Local Restaurants: Exploring Regional Specialties

Beyond hawker centers and Mamak restaurants, Malaysia boasts a diverse array of local restaurants serving regional specialties and ethnic cuisines. Venture into different neighborhoods to discover hidden culinary gems and savor the unique flavors of each region.

Here are some types of local restaurants to explore:

- **Malay Restaurants:** Offering traditional Malay dishes, from spicy curries to fragrant rice dishes and fresh seafood.

- **Chinese Restaurants:** Serving a variety of Chinese cuisines, including Cantonese, Hokkien, and Szechuan dishes.

- **Indian Restaurants:** From North Indian curries and tandoori dishes to South Indian vegetarian fare, explore the diverse flavors of Indian cuisine.

- **Nyonya Restaurants:** Serving Peranakan (Straits Chinese) cuisine, a unique blend of Chinese and Malay influences.

Fine Dining: Elevated Culinary Experiences

For a more refined dining experience, Malaysia offers a growing number of fine dining restaurants, helmed by acclaimed chefs who are pushing the boundaries of Malaysian cuisine and showcasing innovative culinary creations. These restaurants often source premium ingredients, utilize modern cooking techniques, and offer impeccable service.

Tips for Navigating the Food Scene: Embracing the Culinary Adventure

Here are some essential tips for navigating the food scene in Malaysia and making the most of your culinary adventure:

- **Be Adventurous:** Don't be afraid to step outside your comfort zone and try new dishes. You'll be surprised by the variety and deliciousness of Malaysian cuisine.

- **Ask for Recommendations:** Ask locals for their favorite food stalls or restaurants. They often know the best hidden gems and can guide you to authentic local flavors.

- **Use Food Delivery Apps:** Food delivery apps like GrabFood and Foodpanda offer a convenient way to order meals from a wide range of restaurants and have them delivered to your doorstep.

- **Learn Some Basic Malay Food Terms:** Knowing a few basic Malay food terms, such as "nasi" (rice), "ayam" (chicken), "ikan" (fish), "pedas" (spicy), and "manis" (sweet), can be helpful when ordering food.

- **Practice Good Food Hygiene:** Choose reputable eateries and ensure that the food is prepared and handled hygienically. Avoid raw or undercooked food, especially shellfish.

- **Carry Cash:** While credit cards are accepted at many restaurants, it's advisable to carry cash, particularly for smaller food stalls or hawker centers.

A Culinary Journey to Remember: Savor the Flavors of Malaysia

Moving to Malaysia is an invitation to embark on a culinary journey that will tantalize your taste buds, expand your palate, and leave you with unforgettable gastronomic memories. Embrace the country's rich food culture, explore its diverse culinary offerings, and savor the flavors that make Malaysia a true food lover's paradise.

CHAPTER FOURTEEN: Shopping and Entertainment in Malaysia

Moving to a new country can feel a bit like stepping into a whirlwind of unfamiliar sights and sounds. But once the initial flurry of settling in subsides, you'll be eager to explore your new surroundings, discover hidden gems, and experience all that Malaysia has to offer. And what better way to do that than through its vibrant shopping and entertainment scene!

Malaysia is a shopper's paradise, offering a delightful blend of modern megamalls, bustling street markets, quirky independent boutiques, and traditional craft shops. Whether you're seeking designer brands, local handicrafts, or just a fun day out browsing for unique finds, Malaysia has something to satisfy every shopping urge. And when the shopping bags are full, the entertainment options are just as diverse, from world-class cinemas and live music venues to thrilling theme parks and cultural performances. This chapter will guide you through the shopping and entertainment landscape of Malaysia, helping you uncover the best spots, snag great deals, and create unforgettable experiences.

Shopping in Malaysia: A Shopaholic's Delight

From high-end malls to bargain-filled night markets, Malaysia offers a kaleidoscope of shopping experiences to suit every taste and budget.

Malls: Where Shopping Meets Entertainment

Malaysia is renowned for its megamalls, sprawling air-conditioned havens that offer a dazzling array of shopping, dining, and entertainment options under one roof. These malls are more than just places to shop; they are social hubs, entertainment destinations, and even architectural marvels.

Here's what you can expect to find in Malaysian malls:

- **Fashion and Apparel:** From international luxury brands to local designer labels and affordable fast fashion, Malaysian malls cater to a wide range of tastes and budgets. You'll find everything from designer handbags and shoes to trendy clothing, sportswear, and accessories.

- **Electronics and Gadgets:** Malaysia is a major hub for electronics manufacturing, so you'll find a wide selection of the latest gadgets, smartphones, laptops, cameras, and home appliances at competitive prices. Check out major electronics retailers like Harvey Norman, Senheng, and Courts for great deals.

- **Homeware and Furniture:** Whether you're furnishing your new Malaysian home or just looking for stylish home décor items, Malaysian malls offer a wide range of options, from modern minimalist furniture to traditional handcrafted pieces.

- **Books and Stationery:** Bookworms rejoice! Malaysian malls are home to major bookstore chains like MPH, Popular, and Kinokuniya, offering a wide selection of books, magazines, stationery, and gifts.

- **Supermarkets and Department Stores:** Malls also have large supermarkets and department stores, such as AEON, Tesco, and Giant, where you can stock up on groceries, household essentials, and other everyday items.

Popular Malls: From Iconic Landmarks to Neighborhood Gems

Mall	Location	Highlights
Suria KLCC	Kuala Lumpur City Centre (KLCC)	Located at the base of the iconic Petronas Twin Towers, Suria KLCC is a luxurious mall offering high-end brands, fine dining restaurants, a concert hall, and an art gallery.

Pavilion Kuala Lumpur	Bukit Bintang, Kuala Lumpur	A stylish mall with a mix of luxury brands, high-street fashion, and a wide selection of dining and entertainment options.
Mid Valley Megamall	Mid Valley City, Kuala Lumpur	One of the largest malls in Southeast Asia, Mid Valley Megamall offers a vast array of shops, restaurants, a cinema, a bowling alley, and an exhibition center.
1 Utama Shopping Centre	Bandar Utama, Petaling Jaya	Another sprawling megamall, 1 Utama boasts a wide selection of shops, an indoor rainforest, a rock-climbing wall, and an ice-skating rink.
Gurney Plaza	Gurney Drive, Penang	A popular mall in Penang, offering a mix of international and local brands, a cinema, and a variety of dining options.
Queensbay Mall	Bayan Lepas, Penang	A large mall with a focus on family entertainment, Queensbay Mall boasts a theme park, a water park, a cinema, and a bowling alley.
Paradigm Mall Johor Bahru	Skudai, Johor Bahru	A modern mall with a wide selection of shops, restaurants, a cinema, and an ice-skating rink.

Street Markets: A Sensory Overload of Sights, Sounds, and Smells

For a more authentic and immersive shopping experience, venture into the bustling street markets that come alive in many Malaysian towns and cities, particularly in the evenings. These markets are a sensory overload of sights, sounds, and smells, offering a glimpse into the local way of life and a chance to snag some unique finds at bargain prices.

Here's what you can expect to find in Malaysian street markets:

- **Clothing and Accessories:** From trendy fashion items to traditional clothing, shoes, and accessories, street markets offer a wide variety of styles at affordable prices. Be prepared to bargain for the best deals.

- **Food and Snacks:** Street markets are a food lover's paradise, with a tempting array of local snacks, desserts, and street food, often cooked fresh right in front of you.

- **Fresh Produce and Seafood:** Some street markets also have sections selling fresh fruits, vegetables, and seafood, offering a chance to experience the local produce and interact with vendors.

- **Handicrafts and Souvenirs:** Looking for unique souvenirs or traditional handicrafts? Street markets are a great place to find handcrafted items, such as batik fabrics, wood carvings, and traditional jewelry, often made by local artisans.

- **Electronics and Gadgets:** You might be surprised to find electronics and gadgets at street markets, often at lower prices than in malls. However, exercise caution and ensure the products are genuine before making a purchase.

Popular Street Markets: A Glimpse into Local Life

Market	Location	Highlights
Petaling Street Market (Chinatown)	Kuala Lumpur	A bustling market in Kuala Lumpur's Chinatown, known for its wide selection of clothing, accessories, souvenirs, and street food.
Central Market (Pasar Seni)	Kuala Lumpur	A historic market building, now a popular tourist destination offering handicrafts, souvenirs, art galleries, and cultural performances.
Jalan Alor Night	Bukit Bintang,	A famous street food destination, Jalan Alor comes alive at night with a dazzling array of food

Market	Kuala Lumpur	stalls serving local delicacies.
Lorong Kulit Flea Market	George Town, Penang	A lively flea market with a vintage vibe, offering antiques, collectibles, vintage clothing, and street food.
Chulia Street Night Market	George Town, Penang	A popular night market with a mix of clothing, accessories, souvenirs, and street food, particularly known for its Indian Muslim food stalls.
Jonker Street Night Market	Malacca	Held every Friday and Saturday night, Jonker Street transforms into a bustling night market offering antiques, souvenirs, clothing, and a variety of local snacks.

Independent Boutiques and Craft Shops: Discovering Unique Treasures

Beyond the mainstream shopping malls and bustling street markets, Malaysia has a thriving scene of independent boutiques and craft shops, offering a curated selection of unique and locally made products. These shops are often a treasure trove of one-of-a-kind finds, from designer clothing and accessories to handcrafted jewelry, home décor, and art pieces.

Here's where to discover these hidden gems:

- **Heritage Neighborhoods:** Explore heritage neighborhoods like George Town in Penang, Jonker Street in Malacca, and Bangsar in Kuala Lumpur, where you'll find clusters of independent boutiques, art galleries, and craft shops.

- **Online Marketplaces:** Online platforms like Etsy and Pinkoi are great resources for discovering Malaysian artisans and independent designers who sell their products online.

- **Social Media:** Follow local designers and boutiques on social media platforms like Instagram and Facebook to stay updated on their latest collections and events.

- **Craft Markets and Fairs:** Attend craft markets and fairs, often held in community centers, parks, or shopping malls, to discover locally made products and meet the artisans behind them.

Shopping Tips: Snagging Great Deals and Navigating the Scene

Here are some tips for navigating the shopping scene in Malaysia and making the most of your shopping sprees:

- **Bargaining is Expected:** In street markets and smaller shops, bargaining is a common practice. Don't be shy to negotiate for a better price, but do so politely and respectfully.

- **Check for Quality:** Examine products carefully for quality before making a purchase, especially in street markets where counterfeit goods may be present.

- **Pay in Cash:** While credit cards are accepted at most malls and larger stores, smaller shops and street markets may prefer cash payments.

- **Shop During Sales Seasons:** Malaysia has several major sales seasons throughout the year, such as the Malaysia Mega Sale Carnival, the Year-End Sale, and the Chinese New Year Sale. Shop during these periods for significant discounts.

- **Respect Local Customs:** When entering shops or interacting with vendors, be mindful of local customs and etiquette. Greet the staff with a friendly "Selamat pagi" (good morning), "Selamat tengah hari" (good afternoon), or "Selamat petang" (good evening), depending on the time of day.

- **Enjoy the Experience:** Shopping in Malaysia is not just about acquiring goods but also about experiencing the vibrant atmosphere, interacting with locals, and discovering unique treasures.

Entertainment in Malaysia: From Cinematic Thrills to Cultural Delights

Beyond shopping, Malaysia offers a diverse array of entertainment options to suit every taste and interest.

Cinemas: Catching the Latest Blockbusters

Malaysian cinemas offer a mix of Hollywood blockbusters, international films, and local productions. Major cinema chains like Golden Screen Cinemas (GSC), TGV Cinemas, and MBO Cinemas operate modern multiplexes in major cities and towns, offering comfortable seating, state-of-the-art sound systems, and a variety of snack options.

Ticket prices are generally affordable, ranging from RM10 to RM25, depending on the location, time of day, and type of seating. Online booking platforms make it convenient to reserve your seats in advance.

Live Music: From Indie Bands to International Acts

Malaysia's live music scene is vibrant and diverse, with venues catering to a wide range of genres, from indie rock and jazz to electronic dance music and traditional Malay performances. Major cities like Kuala Lumpur and Penang have a thriving live music scene, with established venues hosting both local and international acts.

Here are some popular live music venues:

- **The Bee, Publika (Kuala Lumpur):** A popular spot for indie bands, acoustic performances, and open mic nights.

- **No Black Tie (Kuala Lumpur):** A renowned jazz club, hosting both local and international jazz musicians.

- **Zouk Club (Kuala Lumpur):** A large nightclub and entertainment complex, hosting international DJs and electronic dance music events.

- **Penang Performing Arts Centre (Penang):** A multi-purpose arts venue, hosting a variety of performances, including live music, dance, and theater.

Theme Parks: Thrills and Spills for All Ages

Malaysia boasts several theme parks and amusement parks, offering thrills and spills for all ages. From roller coasters and water slides to interactive exhibits and animal encounters, theme parks are a fun day out for families, couples, and thrill-seekers alike.

Here are some popular theme parks in Malaysia:

- **Sunway Lagoon (Petaling Jaya):** A large theme park with six different zones, including a water park, an amusement park, a wildlife park, and a scream park.

- **Genting Highlands Theme Park (Genting Highlands):** Located in the cool mountain resort of Genting Highlands, this theme park offers a mix of indoor and outdoor rides, as well as a casino and entertainment complex.

- **Legoland Malaysia (Johor Bahru):** A theme park dedicated to the iconic Lego bricks, featuring rides, shows, and interactive exhibits.

- **Lost World of Tambun (Ipoh):** A theme park with a water park, an amusement park, a petting zoo, and hot springs.

Cultural Performances: A Glimpse into Traditional Arts

Immerse yourself in the richness of Malaysian culture by attending traditional dance performances, musical shows, or theatrical productions. Cultural centers, theaters, and even some shopping malls host cultural performances that showcase the diverse artistic heritage of Malaysia.

Here are some places to experience cultural performances:

- **Istana Budaya (Kuala Lumpur):** The national theater of Malaysia, hosting a variety of traditional and contemporary performances.

- **Petronas Philharmonic Hall (Kuala Lumpur):** Home to the Malaysian Philharmonic Orchestra, hosting classical music concerts and other performances.

- **Penang Performing Arts Centre (Penang):** A multi-purpose arts venue, hosting a range of cultural performances, from traditional dance to contemporary theater.

Nightlife: Bars, Clubs, and Entertainment Hubs

Malaysia's nightlife scene caters to a wide range of tastes, from laid-back bars and pubs to high-energy nightclubs and rooftop lounges. Major cities like Kuala Lumpur, Penang, and Johor Bahru offer a vibrant nightlife, with entertainment hubs attracting both locals and expats.

Here are some popular nightlife areas:

- **Changkat Bukit Bintang (Kuala Lumpur):** A lively street lined with bars, pubs, restaurants, and nightclubs.

- **Jalan P. Ramlee (Kuala Lumpur):** Another popular nightlife destination, known for its upscale clubs and lounges.

- **Gurney Drive (Penang):** A coastal promenade with a mix of bars, restaurants, and nightclubs, offering stunning sea views.

Other Entertainment Options: Exploring Your Interests

Beyond the mainstream entertainment options, Malaysia offers a plethora of activities and attractions to explore, depending on your interests:

- **Sports:** Catch a football match, watch a badminton tournament, or play a round of golf at one of Malaysia's many golf courses.

- **Nature and Adventure:** Go hiking in the rainforest, explore caves, or enjoy watersports activities like diving, snorkeling, and sailing.

- **Museums and Art Galleries:** Immerse yourself in history and art at museums and galleries throughout the country.

- **Spas and Wellness:** Pamper yourself with a massage, spa treatment, or a traditional Malay healing experience.

Entertainment Tips: Making the Most of Your Leisure Time

Here are some tips for enjoying the entertainment scene in Malaysia:

- **Check Event Listings:** Stay updated on upcoming events, concerts, and performances by checking online event listings, local newspapers, and social media.

- **Book Tickets in Advance:** For popular events or performances, it's advisable to book tickets in advance to avoid disappointment.

- **Embrace Local Experiences:** Explore traditional Malaysian entertainment options, such as wayang kulit (shadow puppet theater), gamelan (traditional orchestra), or silat (Malay martial art).

- **Be Open to New Experiences:** Step outside your comfort zone and try something new, whether it's a different genre of music, a cultural performance, or an adventurous activity.

- **Have Fun!** Malaysia's entertainment scene is diverse and vibrant, offering something for everyone. Relax, enjoy yourself, and make the most of your leisure time.

CHAPTER FIFTEEN: Travel and Tourism: Exploring Malaysia's Beauty

Moving to Malaysia opens the door to a world of travel and adventure. This Southeast Asian gem is blessed with a tapestry of natural wonders, vibrant cities, charming towns, and a rich cultural heritage that beckons exploration. Whether you're a nature enthusiast seeking pristine beaches and lush rainforests, a history buff intrigued by ancient temples and colonial architecture, a foodie eager to savor regional delicacies, or an adrenaline junkie craving thrilling outdoor adventures, Malaysia has something to offer every traveler.

This chapter will serve as your guide to uncovering the best of Malaysia's travel destinations, from iconic landmarks and hidden gems to off-the-beaten-path adventures and cultural experiences. We'll delve into the diverse regions, highlight must-visit attractions, provide practical travel tips, and inspire you to create unforgettable memories as you explore the beauty of your new home.

Peninsular Malaysia: A Tapestry of Contrasts

Peninsular Malaysia, the western half of the country, offers a captivating blend of modern cities, historical towns, idyllic islands, and lush rainforests.

Kuala Lumpur: A Metropolis of Modernity and Heritage

Kuala Lumpur, the bustling capital city, is a dynamic metropolis that seamlessly blends modern skyscrapers with historical landmarks, creating a unique urban landscape.

Iconic Landmarks:

- **Petronas Twin Towers:** Once the tallest buildings in the world, the Petronas Twin Towers are an architectural marvel, soaring 452 meters into the sky. Take a guided tour to the Skybridge for breathtaking views of the city or visit the Petronas Art Gallery for a dose of culture.

- **Batu Caves:** A sacred Hindu site, the Batu Caves are a complex of limestone caves, home to temples and shrines. Climb the 272 colorful steps to reach the main cave, where you'll be greeted by a towering golden statue of Lord Murugan.

- **KL Tower:** Standing at 421 meters, the KL Tower offers panoramic views of the city. Enjoy a revolving restaurant experience or opt for a thrilling skywalk on the open-air observation deck.

- **Merdeka Square:** A historical landmark, Merdeka Square marks the spot where Malaysia declared its independence in 1957. Admire the colonial-era buildings surrounding the square, including the Sultan Abdul Samad Building and the Royal Selangor Club.

Cultural Experiences:

- **Central Market (Pasar Seni):** Housed in a historic Art Deco building, Central Market is a vibrant hub for arts, crafts, and cultural performances. Browse for souvenirs, admire traditional handicrafts, or catch a live music show.

- **Chinatown (Petaling Street):** Experience the hustle and bustle of Kuala Lumpur's Chinatown, with its street markets, traditional shophouses, and Chinese temples. Sample local delicacies, bargain for souvenirs, or enjoy a traditional Chinese tea ceremony.

- **Little India (Brickfields):** Immerse yourself in the sights, sounds, and aromas of Little India, with its colorful shops, temples, and restaurants serving authentic Indian cuisine.

Nature Escapes:

- **KL Forest Eco Park:** Escape the urban jungle and immerse yourself in nature at KL Forest Eco Park, a rainforest reserve within the city limits. Hike through the canopy walkway for a bird's-eye view or explore the nature trails.

- **Lake Gardens:** A sprawling green oasis in the heart of Kuala Lumpur, Lake Gardens offers a serene escape from the city's hustle and bustle. Stroll through the gardens, admire the colorful orchids, or rent a boat for a leisurely ride on the lake.

Malacca: A Historical Journey Through Time

Malacca, a UNESCO World Heritage City on the southwestern coast of Peninsular Malaysia, is steeped in history, a testament to its past as a major trading port. Explore its colonial architecture, ancient temples, and cultural landmarks, a journey through time that reveals the influences of Malay, Portuguese, Dutch, and British rule.

Historical Landmarks:

- **A Famosa:** Built by the Portuguese in the 16th century, A Famosa is a historical fortress, a reminder of Malacca's colonial past. Explore the remaining gatehouse, a symbol of the city's resilience.

- **St. Paul's Church:** A ruined church atop St. Paul's Hill, offering panoramic views of the city. Explore the ruins, admire the tombstones of Dutch dignitaries, and learn about the history of Christianity in Malacca.

- **Christ Church:** A distinctive red-brick church, built by the Dutch in the 18th century, a symbol of Malacca's Dutch colonial heritage. Admire the interior, featuring Dutch tombstones and a hand-carved pulpit.

- **Stadthuys:** The former Dutch administrative building, now a museum showcasing Malacca's history and culture.

Cultural Experiences:

- **Jonker Street:** A historic street lined with traditional shophouses, antique shops, art galleries, and restaurants. Browse for souvenirs, sample local delicacies, or enjoy a traditional Nyonya (Straits Chinese) meal.

- **Baba Nyonya Heritage Museum:** Step into the world of the Peranakan (Straits Chinese) community at the Baba Nyonya Heritage Museum, a beautifully preserved traditional townhouse that showcases their unique culture, traditions, and exquisite craftsmanship.

River Cruise: Take a relaxing river cruise along the Malacca River, enjoying views of the city's historical landmarks and charming water villages.

Penang: The Pearl of the Orient

Penang, an island state off the northwest coast of Peninsular Malaysia, is a captivating blend of colonial charm, vibrant street art, and a tantalizing culinary scene.

Historical Landmarks:

- **George Town:** A UNESCO World Heritage City, George Town is a fascinating mix of colonial architecture, traditional shophouses, Chinese temples, and vibrant street art. Explore the historic streets, admire the intricate murals, and sample the city's famous street food.

- **Cheong Fatt Tze - The Blue Mansion:** A stunning indigo-blue mansion, built in the late 19th century by a wealthy Chinese businessman. Take a guided tour to admire the intricate architecture, learn about its history, and experience the grandeur of this unique heritage building.

- **Kek Lok Si Temple:** One of the largest Buddhist temples in Southeast Asia, Kek Lok Si Temple is a magnificent complex of temples, pagodas, and gardens, a symbol of Penang's Chinese heritage. Admire the intricate architecture, the towering statue of Guanyin (Goddess of Mercy), and the serene atmosphere.

Cultural Experiences:

- **Penang Hill Funicular Railway:** Take a scenic ride on the Penang Hill Funicular Railway to the summit of Penang Hill, enjoying breathtaking views of the island and the mainland. Explore the nature trails, visit the temples, or enjoy a meal at one of the restaurants with stunning vistas.

- **Khoo Kongsi:** A magnificent clan house, built by the wealthy Khoo family in the 19th century. Admire the intricate carvings, the ornate decorations, and the ancestral hall, a testament to Penang's Chinese heritage.

Beach Escapes:

- **Batu Ferringhi:** A popular beach destination on the north coast of Penang, Batu Ferringhi offers a mix of resorts, hotels, restaurants, watersports activities, and a lively night market.

- **Tanjung Bungah:** A more tranquil beach area, Tanjung Bungah offers a mix of luxury resorts, boutique hotels, and charming cafes, ideal for a relaxing getaway.

Cameron Highlands: A Cool Mountain Retreat

Escape the tropical heat and head to the Cameron Highlands, a cool mountain resort in the heart of Peninsular Malaysia. Known for its tea plantations, strawberry farms, and refreshing climate, the Cameron Highlands offer a tranquil escape from the hustle and bustle of city life.

Nature Experiences:

- **Tea Plantations:** Visit the sprawling tea plantations that blanket the hillsides, enjoy a scenic tea-tasting session, and learn about the process of tea production.

- **Strawberry Farms:** Pick your own strawberries at one of the many strawberry farms in the Cameron Highlands, a fun activity for families and fruit lovers alike.

- **Mossy Forest:** Explore the mystical Mossy Forest, a unique ecosystem shrouded in mist and covered in moss, ferns, and orchids. Hike through the trails, admire the ancient trees, and enjoy the refreshing cool air.

- **Waterfalls:** Discover the cascading waterfalls hidden amidst the rainforest, such as Robinson Falls and Parit Falls, perfect spots for a refreshing dip or a picnic.

Hiking and Trekking: The Cameron Highlands offer a variety of hiking and trekking trails, ranging from easy nature walks to challenging summit climbs. Explore the trails, admire the stunning views, and immerse yourself in the tranquility of nature.

Taman Negara: A Rainforest Adventure

Embark on a rainforest adventure in Taman Negara, one of the oldest rainforests in the world. Located in the heart of Peninsular Malaysia, Taman Negara offers a chance to experience the wonders of nature, from towering trees and cascading waterfalls to diverse wildlife and unique plant life.

Nature Experiences:

- **Canopy Walkway:** Walk among the treetops on the world's longest canopy walkway, suspended 40 meters above the forest floor. Enjoy breathtaking views of the rainforest and spot wildlife.

- **Jungle Trekking:** Explore the rainforest trails, ranging from short nature walks to multi-day treks, guided by experienced local guides. Discover hidden waterfalls, ancient trees, and fascinating flora and fauna.

- **Night Safari:** Venture into the rainforest after dark on a night safari, a chance to spot nocturnal animals, such as civet cats, owls, and insects.

- **River Cruise:** Take a relaxing river cruise along the Tembeling River, enjoying views of the rainforest, the traditional villages, and the diverse wildlife.

Tioman Island: A Diver's Paradise

Escape to Tioman Island, a tropical paradise off the east coast of Peninsular Malaysia, renowned for its pristine beaches, crystal-clear waters, and diverse marine life.

Beach Escapes:

- **Juara Beach:** A secluded beach on the east coast of Tioman Island, known for its tranquility, stunning sunsets, and surf breaks.

- **Salang Beach:** A popular beach with a lively atmosphere, offering a variety of restaurants, bars, and watersports activities.

- **Monkey Bay:** A picturesque bay, home to a playful troop of monkeys, a fun spot for swimming, snorkeling, and relaxing on the beach.

Diving and Snorkeling: Tioman Island is a diver's paradise, with numerous dive sites offering a chance to explore coral reefs, shipwrecks, and a diverse array of marine life, from colorful fish to turtles and sharks. Snorkeling is also a popular activity, with shallow reefs easily accessible from the shore.

East Malaysia (Borneo): Untamed Beauty and Cultural Encounters

East Malaysia, encompassing the states of Sabah and Sarawak on the island of Borneo, offers a world of untamed beauty, adventure, and cultural encounters. Explore its pristine rainforests, encounter unique wildlife, discover ancient caves, and immerse yourself in the traditions of the indigenous communities.

Sabah: Land Below the Wind

Sabah, known as the "Land Below the Wind" due to its location below the typhoon belt, is a state of diverse landscapes, from towering mountains and lush rainforests to pristine beaches and vibrant coral reefs.

Nature Experiences:

- **Mount Kinabalu:** Climb Southeast Asia's highest peak, Mount Kinabalu, a challenging but rewarding trek that offers breathtaking views of Sabah's diverse landscapes.

- **Kinabatangan River:** Take a river cruise along the Kinabatangan River, one of the longest rivers in Malaysia, and spot wildlife, including orangutans, proboscis monkeys, elephants, and crocodiles.

- **Danum Valley Conservation Area:** Explore the pristine rainforest of Danum Valley, a protected area teeming with biodiversity, from ancient trees to rare birds and mammals.

- **Sipadan Island:** A world-renowned diving destination, Sipadan Island boasts a rich marine ecosystem, with diverse coral reefs, schools of fish, turtles, and sharks.

Cultural Encounters:

- **Mari Mari Cultural Village:** Experience the traditions and lifestyle of Sabah's indigenous communities at the Mari Mari Cultural Village, a living museum where you can learn about their customs, crafts, and traditional dances.

Sarawak: Land of the Hornbills

Sarawak, the largest state in Malaysia, is known as the "Land of the Hornbills," a reference to the majestic birds that are a symbol of the state. Explore its rainforests, discover ancient caves, and immerse yourself in the cultural heritage of its diverse indigenous communities.

Nature Experiences:

- **Gunung Mulu National Park:** A UNESCO World Heritage Site, Gunung Mulu National Park is home to stunning limestone caves, including the Sarawak Chamber, the largest cave chamber in the world by surface area. Explore the caves, admire the unique rock formations, and encounter the diverse cave fauna.

- **Bako National Park:** A coastal national park with diverse ecosystems, from rocky cliffs to mangrove forests and beaches. Hike through the trails, spot wildlife, including proboscis monkeys and silver leaf monkeys, and enjoy the stunning coastal scenery.

- **Niah National Park:** Home to the Niah Caves, an archaeological site with evidence of human habitation dating back 40,000 years. Explore the caves, learn about their history, and admire the unique rock formations.

Cultural Encounters:

- **Sarawak Cultural Village:** A living museum that showcases the traditions and lifestyle of Sarawak's diverse indigenous communities. Experience their cultural performances, learn about their crafts, and sample their traditional cuisine.

Travel Tips: Planning Your Malaysian Adventures

Here are some practical tips for planning your travels in Malaysia:

- **Best Time to Visit:** Malaysia has a tropical climate, with warm temperatures and high humidity year-round. The best time to visit depends on the region and your interests. The west coast of Peninsular Malaysia is generally drier from December to February, while the east coast is best visited from April to October. Borneo can be visited year-round, although rainfall is more frequent during the monsoon seasons (November to March and May to September).

- **Visas:** Most nationalities can enter Malaysia visa-free for tourism purposes for periods ranging from 14 to 90 days, depending on your citizenship. Check the latest visa requirements on the official website of the Malaysian Immigration Department.

- **Transportation:** Malaysia has a well-developed transportation system, with options including domestic flights, trains, buses, ferries, taxis, and ride-hailing services. Choose the mode of transportation that best suits your budget, travel style, and destination.

- **Accommodation:** Malaysia offers a wide range of accommodation options, from budget-friendly guesthouses and hostels to luxurious resorts and boutique hotels. Book your accommodations in advance, especially during peak season.

- **Food and Drink:** Malaysia is a food lover's paradise, with diverse culinary offerings to satisfy every palate. Be adventurous, try local dishes, and explore the various culinary experiences, from hawker centers and street food stalls to fine dining restaurants.

- **Health and Safety:** Malaysia is generally a safe country to travel in, but it's always advisable to take precautions to protect your health and safety. Pack a basic first-aid kit, drink bottled water, and be aware of your surroundings.

- **Respect Local Customs:** Be mindful of local customs and traditions, dress modestly when visiting religious sites, and greet people with a friendly "Selamat pagi" (good morning), "Selamat tengah hari" (good afternoon), or "Selamat petang" (good evening), depending on the time of day.

- **Learn Some Basic Malay Phrases:** Knowing a few basic Malay phrases, such as greetings, simple questions, and numbers, can be helpful when interacting with locals.

- **Embrace the Adventure:** Be open to new experiences, immerse yourself in the local culture, and enjoy the journey of discovering the beauty of Malaysia.

CHAPTER SIXTEEN: Nature and Wildlife: Experiencing Malaysia's Biodiversity

Moving to Malaysia is like stepping into a vibrant, living nature documentary. This Southeast Asian nation is a biodiversity hotspot, teeming with a kaleidoscope of life, from lush rainforests and pristine beaches to soaring mountains and mysterious caves. Whether you're an avid hiker, a wildlife enthusiast, a nature photographer, or simply someone who appreciates the beauty of the natural world, Malaysia offers an unparalleled opportunity to connect with nature and witness the wonders of biodiversity firsthand.

This chapter will delve into the remarkable natural landscapes and wildlife that make Malaysia so unique, exploring its diverse ecosystems, highlighting iconic species, and offering tips for experiencing and appreciating the country's natural treasures responsibly and sustainably.

Rainforests: Ancient Ecosystems Teeming with Life

Malaysia's rainforests are among the oldest and most biodiverse ecosystems on Earth, dating back over 130 million years. These lush, verdant jungles are a symphony of life, with towering trees forming a dense canopy, sunlight filtering through the leaves, and a chorus of insects, birds, and animals echoing through the air.

Exploring the Rainforest: A Sensory Adventure

Stepping into a Malaysian rainforest is a sensory immersion like no other. The air is thick with humidity, the scent of damp earth and decaying leaves mingling with the sweet fragrance of tropical flowers. Sunlight dapples through the canopy, casting intricate shadows on the forest floor. The sound of cicadas chirping and birds calling fills the air, punctuated by the occasional rustle of leaves as an unseen creature moves through the undergrowth.

Biodiversity at Its Finest: A Web of Life

Malaysian rainforests are home to an astonishing array of plant and animal life, a testament to the country's position as a biodiversity hotspot. Within a single hectare of rainforest, you might find hundreds of different tree species, a kaleidoscope of orchids, ferns, and mosses, and a diverse array of insects, birds, mammals, and reptiles, all interconnected in a delicate web of life.

Iconic Rainforest Species: Encounters with Nature's Wonders

Here are some of the iconic rainforest species you might encounter on your Malaysian adventures:

- **Orangutans:** These gentle, intelligent apes are found in the rainforests of Borneo (Sabah and Sarawak), swinging through the trees and foraging for fruits and leaves. Witnessing an orangutan in its natural habitat is a truly unforgettable experience.

- **Proboscis Monkeys:** Endemic to Borneo, proboscis monkeys are easily recognizable by their large, bulbous noses, which are more prominent in males. These social monkeys are often seen in groups, feeding on leaves and fruits along riverbanks.

- **Malayan Tigers:** Malaysia is one of the few remaining strongholds for the critically endangered Malayan tiger, a majestic predator that roams the dense jungles of Peninsular Malaysia. While sightings are rare, their presence is a testament to the importance of rainforest conservation.

- **Hornbills:** These large, colorful birds are iconic symbols of the rainforest, their distinctive calls echoing through the canopy. Sarawak is particularly known as the "Land of the Hornbills," with eight hornbill species found in the state.

- **Rafflesia:** The world's largest flower, the Rafflesia, is a parasitic plant that blooms on the forest floor, emitting a pungent odor to attract pollinating insects. Witnessing a Rafflesia in bloom is a rare and remarkable sight.

Threats to the Rainforest: The Importance of Conservation

Malaysia's rainforests face numerous threats, including deforestation, habitat loss, and illegal wildlife trade. Palm oil plantations, logging, and infrastructure development have encroached upon vast areas of rainforest, fragmenting habitats and endangering wildlife.

Conservation efforts are crucial for protecting these invaluable ecosystems and the species that depend on them. Organizations like the World Wide Fund for Nature (WWF) and the Malaysian Nature Society (MNS) are working tirelessly to conserve rainforests, promote sustainable practices, and raise awareness about the importance of biodiversity.

Responsible Rainforest Exploration: Minimizing Your Impact

As you venture into Malaysia's rainforests, it's essential to explore responsibly and minimize your impact on these delicate ecosystems. Here are some tips for responsible rainforest exploration:

- **Choose Reputable Tour Operators:** Select tour operators who prioritize sustainability, minimize environmental impact, and support local communities.

- **Stay on Marked Trails:** Avoid venturing off designated trails, as this can damage fragile vegetation and disturb wildlife habitats.

- **Respect Wildlife:** Observe animals from a safe distance, avoid making loud noises, and never attempt to feed or touch them.

- **Pack Out Your Trash:** Carry all your trash out of the rainforest with you, leaving no trace of your visit.

- **Support Local Conservation Efforts:** Consider donating to organizations working to conserve rainforests and protect wildlife.

Mountains: Soaring Peaks and Breathtaking Views

Malaysia's mountains offer a different perspective on the country's natural beauty, with soaring peaks, rugged landscapes, and breathtaking views.

Mount Kinabalu: Southeast Asia's Highest Peak

Mount Kinabalu, located in Sabah, Borneo, is Southeast Asia's highest peak, rising 4,095 meters above sea level. Climbing Mount Kinabalu is a challenging but rewarding adventure, requiring a permit and a two-day trek. The climb takes you through diverse ecosystems, from lowland rainforest to montane forest and alpine meadows, culminating in a breathtaking sunrise view from the summit.

Cameron Highlands: A Cool Mountain Retreat

The Cameron Highlands, a mountain resort in Peninsular Malaysia, offer a welcome respite from the tropical heat. Known for their tea plantations, strawberry farms, and refreshing climate, the Cameron Highlands offer a tranquil escape from the hustle and bustle of city life. Hike through the trails, explore the mossy forest, or visit a tea plantation for a scenic tea-tasting session.

Genting Highlands: A Mountain Resort with Entertainment Galore

Genting Highlands, another popular mountain resort in Peninsular Malaysia, is known for its entertainment complex, featuring casinos, theme parks, and shopping malls. Take a cable car ride to the summit for stunning views of the surrounding mountains and enjoy the cool mountain air.

Hiking and Trekking: Exploring Mountain Trails

Malaysia offers a diverse range of hiking and trekking trails, from easy nature walks to challenging summit climbs. Explore the trails, admire the stunning views, and immerse yourself in the tranquility of nature. Always check weather conditions, pack appropriate gear, and inform someone of your plans before embarking on a hike.

Beaches: Pristine Shores and Crystal-Clear Waters

Malaysia is blessed with an abundance of stunning beaches, from secluded coves to long stretches of golden sand. Whether you're seeking a relaxing beach getaway, a watersports adventure, or a chance to witness marine life, Malaysia's beaches offer something for everyone.

Popular Beach Destinations: A Coastline of Paradise

Beach Destination	Location	Highlights
Langkawi	Island off the northwest coast of Peninsular Malaysia	Known for its beaches, duty-free shopping, cable car ride to the summit of Gunung Machinchang, and the Langkawi Sky Bridge, a curved pedestrian bridge suspended high above the rainforest.
Perhentian Islands	Islands off the northeast coast of Peninsular Malaysia	Renowned for their pristine beaches, crystal-clear waters, and diverse marine life, ideal for diving, snorkeling, and relaxing beach getaways.
Tioman Island	Island off the east	A popular destination for diving, snorkeling, and beach vacations, with lush rainforests,

	coast of Peninsular Malaysia	waterfalls, and a variety of accommodation options.
Redang Island	Island off the east coast of Peninsular Malaysia	Known for its white sandy beaches, crystal-clear waters, and excellent diving and snorkeling opportunities.
Pangkor Island	Island off the west coast of Peninsular Malaysia	A charming island with a mix of beaches, historical sites, and fishing villages. Explore the Dutch Fort, visit the Fu Lin Kong Temple, or take a boat trip to the nearby Pangkor Laut Island.

Watersports: From Diving to Kayaking

Malaysia's beaches offer a playground for watersports enthusiasts, with opportunities for diving, snorkeling, swimming, kayaking, windsurfing, and more.

- **Diving and Snorkeling:** Malaysia boasts some of the world's best diving and snorkeling sites, with diverse coral reefs, shipwrecks, and a plethora of marine life. Popular diving destinations include Sipadan Island, Redang Island, Perhentian Islands, and Tioman Island.

- **Kayaking and Canoeing:** Explore the coastline, paddle through mangrove forests, or venture into secluded coves by kayak or canoe.

- **Windsurfing and Kitesurfing:** The east coast of Peninsular Malaysia, particularly the islands, offer favorable wind conditions for windsurfing and kitesurfing.

Protecting Marine Life: Sustainable Practices

As you enjoy Malaysia's beaches and watersports activities, it's crucial to be mindful of marine life and protect the fragile ecosystems. Here are some tips for sustainable practices:

- **Use Reef-Safe Sunscreen:** Choose sunscreens that are free of harmful chemicals that can damage coral reefs.

- **Avoid Touching Coral:** Coral reefs are delicate ecosystems that are easily damaged. Avoid touching or standing on coral, and be mindful of your fins when snorkeling or diving.

- **Dispose of Trash Responsibly:** Never litter on the beach or in the ocean. Dispose of your trash properly in designated bins.

- **Support Sustainable Tourism Operators:** Choose tour operators who prioritize sustainability and minimize their impact on the environment.

Caves: Exploring the Subterranean World

Malaysia's limestone formations have created a subterranean world of caves, some of the most impressive and extensive cave systems in Southeast Asia.

Gunung Mulu National Park: A Cave Explorer's Paradise

Gunung Mulu National Park, a UNESCO World Heritage Site in Sarawak, Borneo, is a cave explorer's paradise. It boasts an incredible network of caves, including the Sarawak Chamber, the largest cave chamber in the world by surface area. Explore the caves, admire the unique rock formations, and encounter the diverse cave fauna.

Other Notable Caves: Unveiling the Mysteries of the Underworld

- **Deer Cave (Gunung Mulu National Park):** Home to millions of bats, Deer Cave offers a spectacular sight as the bats emerge from the cave at dusk in a swirling cloud.

- **Lang Cave (Gunung Mulu National Park):** Known for its stunning stalactites and stalagmites, Lang Cave is a must-visit for cave enthusiasts.

- **Gua Tempurung (Perak):** One of the longest caves in Peninsular Malaysia, Gua Tempurung offers a variety of cave tours, from easy walks to challenging climbs.

Responsible Cave Exploration: Preserving the Delicate Ecosystems

Caves are delicate ecosystems, easily damaged by human activity. Explore responsibly and minimize your impact by:

- **Obtaining Permits:** Always obtain the necessary permits before entering caves, and follow the guidelines set by the park authorities.

- **Stay on Marked Trails:** Avoid venturing off designated trails, as this can damage fragile cave formations and disturb cave fauna.

- **Avoid Touching Cave Formations:** Oils from your skin can damage delicate cave formations. Admire them from a distance and avoid touching them.

- **Pack Out Your Trash:** Carry all your trash out of the cave with you, leaving no trace of your visit.

- **Support Cave Conservation Efforts:** Consider donating to organizations working to conserve caves and protect their delicate ecosystems.

Wildlife Encounters: Observing Nature's Wonders

Malaysia's diverse ecosystems support a wealth of wildlife, offering unique opportunities to observe nature's wonders in their natural habitats.

Wildlife Sanctuaries and Conservation Centers: Ethical Encounters

- **Sepilok Orangutan Rehabilitation Centre (Sabah):** Visit the Sepilok Orangutan Rehabilitation Centre, a sanctuary for orphaned and injured orangutans, where you can witness these gentle apes being cared for and rehabilitated before being released back into the wild.

- **Semenggoh Wildlife Centre (Sarawak):** Another orangutan rehabilitation center, Semenggoh Wildlife Centre offers a chance to observe semi-wild orangutans coming to feeding platforms.

- **Kinabatangan Wildlife Sanctuary (Sabah):** Take a river cruise along the Kinabatangan River, home to a diverse array of wildlife, including orangutans, proboscis monkeys, elephants, and crocodiles.

- **Danum Valley Conservation Area (Sabah):** Explore the pristine rainforest of Danum Valley, a protected area teeming with biodiversity, and spot wildlife, including gibbons, clouded leopards, and sun bears.

Wildlife Photography: Capturing the Beauty of Nature

Malaysia is a photographer's dream, with endless opportunities to capture the beauty of nature, from rainforest landscapes and wildlife portraits to stunning sunsets and underwater scenes.

Responsible Wildlife Photography: Ethical Practices

When photographing wildlife, it's essential to prioritize the well-being of the animals and minimize any disturbance. Here are some ethical practices for wildlife photography:

- **Keep Your Distance:** Use a telephoto lens to observe and photograph animals from a safe distance, avoiding any disturbance to their natural behavior.

- **Avoid Using Flash:** Flash photography can startle and disorient animals, particularly nocturnal species. Use natural light whenever possible.

- **Respect Their Habitat:** Never chase or harass animals for a better shot. Respect their habitat and avoid damaging vegetation.

- **Support Conservation Efforts:** Consider donating a portion of your photography earnings to organizations working to protect wildlife.

Embracing Nature: Connecting with Malaysia's Biodiversity

Moving to Malaysia is an opportunity to immerse yourself in the wonders of nature and experience the country's remarkable biodiversity firsthand. Explore its rainforests, mountains, beaches, and caves, encounter unique wildlife, and appreciate the delicate balance of life that makes this Southeast Asian nation so special. By exploring responsibly and supporting conservation efforts, you can help preserve Malaysia's natural treasures for generations to come.

CHAPTER SEVENTEEN: Safety and Security in Malaysia

Moving to a new country, especially one as culturally diverse as Malaysia, always raises questions about safety and security. While Malaysia generally boasts a safe environment for both locals and expats, being informed and taking sensible precautions can significantly enhance your peace of mind and ensure a secure and enjoyable experience. This chapter aims to provide you with a balanced perspective on safety and security in Malaysia, addressing common concerns, outlining potential risks, and offering practical tips for staying safe, navigating potential challenges, and making informed decisions about your well-being.

A Generally Safe Environment: Dispelling Misconceptions

Malaysia, compared to many other countries, has a relatively low crime rate, and violent crime is relatively uncommon. The country's multicultural society, underpinned by a strong sense of community and shared values, contributes to a generally peaceful and harmonious environment.

However, like any other country, Malaysia is not entirely free from crime. Petty theft, scams, and cybercrime are potential risks, particularly in crowded urban areas and tourist hotspots.

Petty Theft: Protecting Your Belongings

Petty theft, such as pickpocketing, bag snatching, and theft from vehicles, can occur, especially in crowded areas like markets, public transportation, and tourist attractions. While these incidents are not as frequent as in some other countries, taking precautions to protect your belongings can significantly reduce your risk.

Here are some tips for safeguarding your valuables:

- **Be Aware of Your Surroundings:** Pay attention to your surroundings, especially in crowded areas or when using public transportation.

- **Keep Valuables Secure:** Don't carry large amounts of cash or display expensive jewelry. Keep your valuables, such as your passport, wallet, and phone, in a secure bag or pocket, close to your body.

- **Don't Leave Belongings Unattended:** Never leave your bags or belongings unattended in public places, such as restaurants, cafes, or shops.

- **Secure Your Vehicle:** When parking your car, ensure all doors are locked and windows are closed. Don't leave valuables visible inside the vehicle.

- **Be Cautious of Strangers:** Be wary of strangers approaching you, particularly those who seem overly friendly or try to distract you.

Scams: Staying Vigilant and Informed

Scams targeting tourists and expats can occur in Malaysia, as in many other countries. These scams can range from simple tricks to more elaborate schemes, often involving distractions, false promises, or counterfeit goods.

Here are some common scams to be aware of:

- **Taxi Scams:** Some taxi drivers may attempt to overcharge or take longer routes, particularly with tourists unfamiliar with the area. Always ensure the taxi meter is turned on before starting your journey, or use ride-hailing services like Grab for a more transparent fare structure.

- **Fake Goods:** Counterfeit goods, such as designer handbags, watches, and electronics, are sometimes sold in street markets or by street vendors. Be cautious of products sold at suspiciously low prices and verify the authenticity of goods before making a purchase.

- **Timeshare Scams:** Be wary of individuals approaching you with offers of free gifts, prizes, or discounts for attending timeshare presentations. These presentations can be high-pressure sales pitches, and the offers may not be as attractive as they seem.

- **Charity Scams:** Be cautious of individuals soliciting donations for charities that may not be legitimate. Verify the authenticity of the charity before donating.

Here are some tips for avoiding scams:

- **Be Skeptical of Unsolicited Offers:** Be wary of unsolicited offers, particularly those that seem too good to be true.

- **Do Your Research:** Before making any purchases or commitments, research prices, products, or services to ensure they are legitimate and fair.

- **Trust Your Instincts:** If something feels off or suspicious, trust your instincts and walk away.

- **Report Scams:** If you encounter a scam, report it to the police or the relevant authorities.

Cybercrime: Protecting Your Digital Life

Cybercrime is a growing concern worldwide, and Malaysia is no exception. Online scams, phishing attacks, and data breaches can target individuals and businesses, compromising personal information and financial security.

Here are some tips for protecting yourself from cybercrime:

- **Use Strong Passwords:** Create strong, unique passwords for all your online accounts, and avoid using the same password for multiple accounts.

- **Be Cautious of Suspicious Emails and Links:** Don't open emails or click on links from unknown senders, as these could be phishing attempts to steal your personal information.

- **Secure Your Devices:** Install antivirus software and keep your operating systems and software updated with the latest security patches.

- **Be Mindful of Public Wi-Fi:** Avoid accessing sensitive information, such as online banking accounts, when using public Wi-Fi, as these networks may not be secure.

- **Report Cybercrime:** If you suspect you have been a victim of cybercrime, report it to the police or the Malaysian Communications and Multimedia Commission (MCMC).

Road Safety: Navigating the Roads with Caution

Road accidents are a significant concern in Malaysia, with a high number of fatalities and injuries each year. While road conditions have improved in recent years, particularly in urban areas, traffic congestion, reckless driving, and road hazards can contribute to accidents.

Here are some tips for staying safe on the roads:

- **Obey Traffic Rules:** Adhere to traffic laws, including speed limits, traffic signals, and lane markings.

- **Be Defensive Driver:** Be aware of other drivers and anticipate potential hazards. Avoid distractions while driving, such as using your mobile phone or eating.

- **Wear Seat Belts:** Always wear seat belts, both as a driver and a passenger.

- **Drive Defensively at Night:** Be extra cautious when driving at night, as visibility can be reduced.

- **Beware of Motorcycles:** Motorcycles are a common mode of transportation in Malaysia, and they often weave through traffic. Be aware of motorcycles when changing lanes or making turns.

- **Avoid Driving Under the Influence:** Never drive under the influence of alcohol or drugs.

- **Plan Your Journeys:** Avoid driving during peak hours, when traffic congestion can be heavy. Use navigation apps like Waze or Google Maps to check traffic conditions and plan your routes.

Natural Disasters: Preparing for the Unexpected

Malaysia is generally not prone to major natural disasters, such as earthquakes or volcanic eruptions. However, the country can experience:

- **Floods:** Heavy rainfall during the monsoon seasons can lead to flooding, particularly in low-lying areas. Stay informed about weather forecasts and be prepared to evacuate if necessary.

- **Landslides:** Heavy rainfall can also trigger landslides, particularly in hilly or mountainous areas. Avoid hiking or driving in areas prone to landslides during periods of heavy rain.

- **Haze:** During the dry season, particularly between June and September, Malaysia can experience haze, caused by forest fires in neighboring Indonesia. The haze can cause respiratory problems, so stay indoors if possible and wear a mask if you need to go outside.

Health and Medical Care: Staying Healthy and Seeking Assistance

Malaysia boasts a well-developed healthcare system, with both public and private options available. However, it's always advisable for expats to take precautions to protect their health and seek medical assistance when needed.

Here are some health and medical care tips:

- **Health Insurance:** Having comprehensive health insurance is crucial for expats in Malaysia, as it provides financial protection against the costs of private healthcare services.

- **Vaccinations:** Consult with your doctor or a travel health clinic before moving to Malaysia to ensure you are up-to-date on necessary vaccinations.

- **Food and Water Safety:** Practice good food hygiene, such as washing hands before meals and choosing reputable eateries. Drink bottled water to avoid potential waterborne illnesses.

- **Mosquito Bites:** Dengue fever is prevalent in Malaysia, particularly during the rainy season. Take precautions to prevent mosquito bites, such as using insect repellent, wearing long sleeves and pants, and eliminating mosquito breeding grounds.

- **Seeking Medical Assistance:** If you experience any health issues, seek medical assistance from a doctor or a hospital. In case of an emergency, dial 999 for an ambulance.

Cultural Sensitivities: Respecting Local Customs

Malaysia is a multicultural society with diverse customs and traditions. Respecting local customs and sensitivities can contribute to a harmonious and respectful environment.

Here are some key cultural considerations:

- **Dress Modestly:** While casual attire is acceptable in most settings, it's advisable to avoid revealing clothing, particularly when visiting religious sites or attending formal events.

- **Respect Religious Practices:** Be mindful of the religious practices of different faiths and avoid engaging in behaviors that may be considered offensive or disrespectful.

- **Avoid Public Displays of Affection:** Public displays of affection, such as kissing or hugging, are generally frowned upon in Malaysia, particularly in conservative areas.

- **Remove Your Shoes:** It's customary to remove your shoes before entering a Malaysian home or a mosque.

- **Use Your Right Hand:** The right hand is considered clean in Malay culture and is used for eating, shaking hands, and giving or receiving items. Avoid using your left hand for these actions.

Staying Informed: Accessing Reliable Information

Staying informed about local news, events, and potential safety concerns can enhance your awareness and help you make informed decisions about your well-being.

Here are some helpful resources:

- **Local News Websites:** Follow reputable local news websites, such as The Star, New Straits Times, and Malay Mail, for current events and news updates.

- **Government Websites:** The Malaysian government's official website (www.malaysia.gov.my) provides information on various aspects of life in Malaysia, including safety and security.

- **Embassy or Consulate:** Your home country's embassy or consulate in Malaysia can provide guidance and assistance in case of emergencies or security concerns.

- **Expat Forums and Groups:** Online forums and social media groups for expats in Malaysia can be valuable sources of information, tips, and advice on safety and security.

Personal Safety Tips: Additional Precautions

Here are some additional personal safety tips to enhance your well-being in Malaysia:

- **Be Aware of Your Surroundings:** Pay attention to your surroundings, especially when walking alone at night or in unfamiliar areas.

- **Walk with Confidence:** Project confidence and avoid appearing lost or vulnerable.

- **Avoid Walking Alone at Night:** If possible, avoid walking alone at night, particularly in poorly lit or isolated areas. Use taxis or ride-hailing services for transportation.

- **Let Someone Know Your Plans:** Inform a friend or family member of your whereabouts, particularly if you're traveling alone or venturing into remote areas.

- **Trust Your Instincts:** If something feels off or suspicious, trust your instincts and remove yourself from the situation.

- **Learn Self-Defense Techniques:** Consider taking self-defense classes to enhance your personal safety skills.

- **Emergency Contacts:** Program emergency contact numbers into your phone, including the police (999), ambulance (999), and your embassy or consulate.

Living in Malaysia offers a safe and secure environment for expats. While petty theft, scams, and cybercrime are potential risks, as in many other countries, taking sensible precautions, staying informed, and respecting local customs can significantly enhance your safety and peace of mind. By embracing these measures, you can focus on enjoying the many wonders and opportunities that this vibrant and welcoming nation has to offer.

CHAPTER EIGHTEEN: Social Life and Making Friends in Malaysia

Moving to a new country can be an exhilarating adventure, but it can also be a bit daunting, especially when it comes to building a new social circle. Leaving behind familiar faces and established friendships can make even the most extroverted person feel a pang of loneliness. But fear not! Malaysia, with its warm and welcoming culture, offers a fertile ground for forging new connections and building lasting friendships.

This chapter will delve into the nuances of social life in Malaysia, exploring the various avenues for meeting people, navigating cultural differences, and building meaningful relationships in your new home.

A Welcoming Culture: Breaking the Ice

Malaysians are generally known for their friendly and hospitable nature. They are often curious about other cultures and eager to welcome newcomers. This inherent warmth makes it relatively easy to strike up conversations, even with strangers. A simple smile, a friendly greeting, or a question about their day can often open the door to a conversation and a potential friendship.

Embracing the Melting Pot: Diversity as a Social Catalyst

Malaysia's multicultural society, with its blend of Malay, Chinese, Indian, and indigenous communities, creates a vibrant social landscape with a plethora of opportunities for cross-cultural interactions. Embrace the chance to learn about different customs, traditions, and perspectives, expanding your social horizons and fostering a deeper understanding of the Malaysian mosaic.

Language: A Bridge to Connection

While English is widely spoken in Malaysia, particularly in urban areas and professional settings, learning some basic Bahasa Malaysia can be a valuable asset in building connections with locals. Even a few phrases, such as greetings, simple questions, and expressions of gratitude, can demonstrate your respect for the local culture and make a positive impression.

Don't be afraid to try speaking Bahasa Malaysia, even if your pronunciation isn't perfect. Most Malaysians will appreciate your effort and be happy to help you along the way.

Finding Your Tribe: Exploring Social Avenues

Building a social circle in a new country takes time and effort. Be proactive in exploring various avenues for meeting people and connecting with those who share your interests. Here are some strategies to consider:

Expat Communities: Finding Familiar Ground

Connecting with other expats can provide a sense of familiarity and support, especially during the initial stages of settling into a new country. Expat communities offer a shared understanding of the challenges and joys of living abroad, and they often organize social events, activities, and support groups that can help you feel more connected.

Here are some ways to connect with expat communities:

- **Online Forums and Social Media Groups:** Online platforms like InterNations, Expat.com, and Facebook groups dedicated to expats in Malaysia provide a virtual space to connect with others, ask questions, share experiences, and find out about social events.

- **Expat Organizations and Clubs:** Many expat organizations and clubs cater to specific nationalities or interests, offering a chance to meet like-minded individuals and engage in social activities.

- **International Schools and Churches:** If you have children attending international schools or are involved in a church community, these can be great places to connect with other expat families.

Workplace Connections: Building Relationships Beyond the Desk

Your workplace can be a natural starting point for building friendships in Malaysia. Take the initiative to get to know your colleagues, engage in conversations during breaks, and accept invitations to social gatherings.

Company events, team outings, and after-work drinks offer opportunities to connect with colleagues in a more relaxed setting, fostering camaraderie and building relationships that extend beyond the workplace.

Hobby Groups and Activities: Connecting Through Shared Interests

Pursuing your hobbies and interests is a fantastic way to meet like-minded individuals who share your passions. Whether you're into sports, arts and crafts, music, photography, or any other activity, Malaysia offers a diverse array of clubs, groups, and classes that cater to a wide range of interests.

Here are some ways to find hobby groups and activities:

- **Meetup.com:** This online platform allows you to search for local groups and events based on your interests.

- **Community Centers and Notice Boards:** Check notice boards at community centers, libraries, and cafes for information about local groups and activities.

- **Social Media:** Search for Facebook groups or Instagram accounts dedicated to your hobbies or interests in your local area.

- **Word of Mouth:** Ask your colleagues, neighbors, or other expats about hobby groups or activities they recommend.

Volunteering: Making a Difference and Connecting with Others

Volunteering your time and skills for a cause you care about is a rewarding way to give back to the community and connect with others who share your values. Malaysia has numerous non-governmental organizations (NGOs) and charitable organizations working in various fields, such as education, environmental conservation, animal welfare, and social services.

Volunteering not only allows you to make a positive impact but also provides opportunities to meet passionate and like-minded individuals from diverse backgrounds.

Language Exchange: Learning and Connecting

Participating in a language exchange is a mutually beneficial way to practice your language skills and connect with someone from a different culture. Find a language exchange partner who is interested in learning your native language, and spend time conversing in both languages, sharing cultural insights and building a friendship.

Social Gatherings and Events: Stepping Out and Meeting New People

Be open to attending social gatherings and events, even if you don't know anyone there. It's a chance to step outside your comfort zone, meet new people, and expand your social circle.

Here are some types of social events to consider:

- **Festivals and Cultural Events:** Malaysia's multicultural society offers a vibrant calendar of festivals and cultural events throughout the year, from religious celebrations to music festivals and art exhibitions. These events are often open to the public and provide a chance to mingle with locals and expats alike.

- **Networking Events:** Professional networking events, organized by industry associations, chambers of commerce, or other organizations, offer opportunities to connect with people in your field and expand your professional circle.

- **Workshops and Classes:** Attend workshops or classes related to your interests, such as cooking classes, dance workshops, or art classes. These activities provide a structured setting to meet people who share your passions.

Sports and Recreation: Bonding over Shared Activities

Sports and recreational activities are a fantastic way to stay active, have fun, and connect with others who share your interests. Whether you're into football, badminton, swimming, running, or any other sport, Malaysia offers a variety of clubs, leagues, and facilities that cater to a wide range of athletic pursuits.

Joining a sports team or a gym can be a great way to meet people, build camaraderie, and stay motivated. Malaysia's beautiful natural landscapes also offer opportunities for outdoor recreation, such as hiking, trekking, cycling, and watersports. Joining a hiking group or a watersports club can be a fun way to explore the country and connect with like-minded individuals.

Navigating Cultural Differences: Building Bridges of Understanding

As you embark on your social journey in Malaysia, remember that cultural differences can sometimes influence social interactions.

Being mindful of these nuances can help you avoid misunderstandings and build stronger relationships.

Respect for Elders and Authority

Malaysian culture places great importance on respect for elders and authority figures. When addressing someone older or of higher status, use the appropriate honorific titles, such as "Encik" (Mr.), "Puan" (Mrs.), or "Cik" (Miss). Avoid being overly familiar or casual in your interactions, particularly in formal settings.

Non-Confrontational Communication

Malaysian communication style tends to be indirect and non-confrontational. Directness and assertiveness, while common in some Western cultures, may be perceived as rude or aggressive in Malaysia. Be mindful of your tone of voice and body language, and try to express your opinions or disagreements politely and diplomatically.

Gift-Giving Etiquette

Gift-giving is a common practice in Malaysia, particularly for special occasions or as a gesture of appreciation. When giving gifts, wrap them neatly and avoid giving gifts that may be considered culturally inappropriate, such as alcohol or pork products to Muslims.

When receiving a gift, accept it with both hands and express your gratitude. It's generally considered polite to open gifts later, in private, unless the giver insists you open it immediately.

Religious Sensitivities

Malaysia is a multi-religious country, with Islam, Buddhism, Christianity, Hinduism, and other faiths coexisting harmoniously. Be respectful of religious sensitivities, dress modestly when visiting religious sites, and avoid making comments that could be interpreted as offensive or disrespectful.

Dining Customs

When dining with Malaysians, wait to be seated by the host, use your right hand for eating, and avoid using your left hand for passing food or utensils. It's considered polite to finish the food on your plate and to express your gratitude to the host for the meal.

Building Meaningful Relationships: Nurturing Friendships

Building strong friendships takes time, effort, and a genuine interest in connecting with others. Here are some tips for nurturing meaningful relationships in Malaysia:

Be Open and Approachable

Approach social interactions with an open mind and a willingness to connect with people from different backgrounds. Smile, be friendly, and initiate conversations. Show genuine interest in getting to know others and learn about their culture and experiences.

Be a Good Listener

Active listening is a crucial skill in building strong relationships. Pay attention to what others are saying, ask follow-up questions, and show empathy. Avoid interrupting or dominating conversations.

Share Your Culture and Experiences

Be open to sharing your own culture and experiences with your Malaysian friends. Share stories about your home country, your family, and your interests. This can help foster a deeper understanding and connection.

Be Patient and Understanding

Building strong friendships takes time. Be patient and understanding, allowing relationships to develop naturally. Don't expect instant intimacy or force connections.

Be Reliable and Supportive

Show your friends that you are reliable and supportive. Be there for them during both happy and challenging times. Offer help when needed and be a good listener when they need someone to talk to.

Respect Boundaries

Respect personal boundaries and cultural differences. Avoid being overly familiar or intrusive. Be mindful of social cues and adjust your behavior accordingly.

Stay Connected

Make an effort to stay connected with your friends, even when life gets busy. Regularly reach out, schedule time to meet up, and stay in touch through phone calls, messages, or social media.

Embracing the Social Tapestry: Weaving New Connections

Building a social life in Malaysia is a rewarding journey of cultural discovery and personal connection. Embrace the country's welcoming culture, explore various social avenues, navigate cultural differences with sensitivity, and nurture meaningful relationships. As you weave new connections into the fabric of your life, you'll find that Malaysia offers not just a new home but also a new community, a place where you can belong, thrive, and create lasting friendships.

CHAPTER NINETEEN: Housing: Renting and Buying Property

Finding the perfect place to call home is a crucial step in settling into your new life in Malaysia. Whether you're envisioning a modern high-rise apartment with panoramic city views, a charming landed house nestled in a leafy suburb, or a tranquil villa by the sea, Malaysia offers a diverse range of housing options to suit every taste, lifestyle, and budget.

This chapter will guide you through the intricacies of the Malaysian housing market, exploring the different types of properties available, the process of renting and buying, legal considerations, financing options, and essential tips for finding your dream home in Malaysia.

Renting in Malaysia: Finding Your Temporary Nest

For many expats, renting is the preferred option, offering flexibility, lower upfront costs, and a chance to experience different neighborhoods before making a long-term commitment. Malaysia's rental market is generally well-established, with a variety of properties available to suit different needs and budgets.

Understanding Property Types

Malaysia offers a diverse range of housing options, from high-rise apartments and condominiums to landed properties, such as terraced houses, semi-detached houses, and bungalows.

Here's a closer look at the different property types:

- **Apartments and Condominiums:** High-rise buildings offering individual units, typically with shared facilities, such as swimming pools, gyms, and security services. Apartments are generally more affordable than landed properties, particularly in urban areas.

- **Terraced Houses (Townhouses):** Rows of houses attached to each other, sharing common walls. Terraced houses typically have two or three stories and offer more space than apartments.

- **Semi-Detached Houses:** Two houses joined together by a common wall, offering more privacy and space than terraced houses.

- **Bungalows:** Detached houses, typically single-story, with larger gardens and more privacy than other types of landed properties. Bungalows are often more expensive than other housing options.

Finding a Rental Property: Resources and Strategies

There are various ways to find rental properties in Malaysia, from online platforms to real estate agents and word-of-mouth referrals:

- **Online Property Portals:** Websites like PropertyGuru, iProperty, and Mudah.my are popular online portals for finding rental properties in Malaysia. You can filter your search by location, price, property type, and other criteria to narrow down your options.

- **Real Estate Agents:** Working with a reputable real estate agent can streamline your property search, as they have access to a wider range of listings and can provide local market insights. They can also handle negotiations, paperwork, and other aspects of the rental process.

- **Word-of-Mouth Referrals:** Ask friends, colleagues, or other expats for recommendations on neighborhoods, properties, or reliable real estate agents.

- **Notice Boards:** Check notice boards at community centers, supermarkets, and other public places for rental property listings.

Viewing Properties: Key Considerations

When viewing potential rental properties, here are some key factors to assess:

- **Location:** Consider the proximity to your workplace, schools, amenities, and transportation options. Traffic congestion can be a significant issue in major cities, so factor in commute times.

- **Safety and Security:** Assess the security features of the property, such as gated access, security guards, and CCTV cameras. Inquire about the safety of the neighborhood.

- **Size and Layout:** Determine if the property's size and layout meet your needs and lifestyle. Consider the number of bedrooms, bathrooms, living spaces, and storage areas.

- **Condition and Amenities:** Check the overall condition of the property, including the appliances, plumbing, and electrical systems. Inquire about the availability of amenities, such as swimming pools, gyms, and parking facilities.

- **Rental Price and Terms:** Negotiate the rental price and terms with the landlord. Clarify the lease duration, security deposit, and payment schedule.

Negotiating the Tenancy Agreement

Once you've found a suitable property, you'll need to negotiate a tenancy agreement with the landlord. The tenancy agreement is a legally binding contract that outlines the terms of the rental, including:

- **Rental Price:** The monthly rental amount.

- **Lease Duration:** The length of the rental period, typically one or two years.

- **Security Deposit:** A refundable deposit, typically equivalent to two or three months' rent, to cover potential damages or unpaid rent.

- **Utilities:** Clarify whether utilities, such as electricity, water, and gas, are included in the rent or if you'll be responsible for paying them separately.

- **Maintenance Responsibilities:** Outline the responsibilities for property maintenance and repairs, such as who is responsible for fixing appliances or handling plumbing issues.

Essential Tips for Renting in Malaysia

Here are some additional tips for navigating the rental market in Malaysia:

- **Be Prepared to Negotiate:** Rental prices are often negotiable, particularly for longer lease terms. Don't be afraid to negotiate with the landlord for a better price.

- **Get Everything in Writing:** Ensure all agreed-upon terms are clearly stated in the tenancy agreement to avoid any misunderstandings or disputes later on.

- **Inspect the Property Thoroughly:** Before signing the tenancy agreement, inspect the property thoroughly and document any existing damages to avoid being held responsible for them at the end of your lease.

- **Pay Your Rent on Time:** Ensure you pay your rent on time to avoid late payment fees or eviction.

- **Communicate with Your Landlord:** Maintain open communication with your landlord regarding any issues or concerns related to the property.

- **Understand Your Rights and Responsibilities:** Familiarize yourself with your rights and responsibilities as a tenant under the Malaysian law.

Buying Property in Malaysia: Investing in Your Future

For expats planning to settle in Malaysia long-term, buying a property can be a wise investment, offering stability, a sense of ownership, and potential capital appreciation. However, navigating the property purchase process in a foreign country can be complex, requiring careful planning, due diligence, and a clear understanding of the legal and financial aspects involved.

Legal Considerations for Foreign Buyers

Foreigners are generally allowed to purchase property in Malaysia, but there are certain restrictions and regulations to be aware of:

- **Minimum Purchase Price:** The Malaysian government has set minimum purchase price requirements for foreign buyers, which vary depending on the type of property and location. These requirements are designed to ensure foreign investment in the property market benefits the local economy.

- **Types of Properties:** Foreigners are generally permitted to purchase residential properties, such as apartments, condominiums, terraced houses, semi-detached houses, and bungalows. However, there may be restrictions on purchasing certain types of properties, such as agricultural land or properties within designated areas.

- **State-Specific Regulations:** Each state in Malaysia may have its own specific regulations regarding foreign property ownership. It's essential to check with the relevant state authorities for the latest guidelines.

Understanding the Purchase Process

The process of buying a property in Malaysia typically involves the following steps:

1. **Property Search:** Identify the type of property, location, and budget that meet your needs. Utilize online property portals, real estate agents, and word-of-mouth referrals to explore available options.

2. **Property Viewing:** View potential properties and assess their suitability, considering factors like location, size, condition, amenities, and price.

3. **Offer to Purchase:** Once you've found a property you're interested in, submit a formal offer to purchase to the seller. The offer typically includes the proposed purchase price and other terms and conditions.

4. **Sale and Purchase Agreement (SPA):** If your offer is accepted, you'll need to sign a Sale and Purchase Agreement (SPA) with the seller. The SPA is a legally binding contract that outlines the terms of the purchase, including the purchase price, payment schedule, and legal obligations of both parties.

5. **Legal Due Diligence:** Engage a lawyer to conduct legal due diligence on the property, verifying ownership, ensuring there are no outstanding debts or encumbrances, and reviewing the SPA.

6. **Loan Application (if applicable):** If you require financing to purchase the property, apply for a mortgage loan from a bank or financial institution.

7. **Payment of Deposit:** Once the SPA is signed, you'll need to pay a deposit, typically 10% of the purchase price.

8. **Completion of Sale:** The final step is the completion of the sale, which involves paying the balance of the purchase price, transferring ownership, and registering the property in your name.

Financing Options: Securing a Mortgage Loan

Foreigners are generally eligible for mortgage loans from Malaysian banks, subject to meeting certain criteria, such as:

- **Minimum Loan Amount:** Banks often have minimum loan amounts for foreign buyers.

- **Loan-to-Value Ratio (LTV):** The LTV ratio represents the percentage of the property value that the bank is willing to finance. Foreign buyers may be subject to lower LTV ratios compared to Malaysian citizens.

- **Interest Rates:** Interest rates on mortgage loans for foreign buyers may be slightly higher than those for citizens.

- **Documentation:** Banks typically require extensive documentation from foreign buyers, including passport copies, visa details, income proof, and bank statements.

Legal Fees and Taxes

Property purchase in Malaysia involves various legal fees and taxes, including:

- **Legal Fees:** You'll need to pay legal fees for your lawyer's services in drafting and reviewing the SPA, conducting due diligence, and handling the property transfer process.

- **Stamp Duty:** Stamp duty is a tax levied on legal documents, including the SPA. The stamp duty rate is based on the purchase price of the property.

- **Real Property Gains Tax (RPGT):** If you sell your property within a certain holding period, you may be subject to RPGT, a tax on the capital gain from the sale.

Essential Tips for Buying Property in Malaysia

Here are some additional tips for navigating the property purchase process in Malaysia:

- **Engage a Reputable Real Estate Agent:** Working with a reputable real estate agent can simplify the process, as they have access to a wider range of listings, can provide local market insights, and can handle negotiations and paperwork.

- **Do Your Research:** Thoroughly research the property market, property prices, neighborhoods, and legal regulations before making any decisions.

- **Seek Legal Advice:** Engage a lawyer who specializes in property transactions to ensure you understand the legal aspects involved and to protect your interests throughout the process.

- **Get a Property Valuation:** Obtain a professional property valuation to ensure you're paying a fair price for the property.

- **Inspect the Property Thoroughly:** Before signing the SPA, thoroughly inspect the property and document any existing defects or issues.

- **Understand the Financing Terms:** If you're taking out a mortgage loan, carefully review the loan terms, interest rates, and repayment schedule to ensure they are favorable and manageable.

Making Informed Decisions: Finding Your Perfect Home

Finding the right housing option in Malaysia, whether you're renting or buying, requires careful consideration of your needs, budget, lifestyle, and long-term goals. By understanding the different property types, the rental and purchase processes, legal regulations, and financing options, you can make informed decisions, navigate the housing market with confidence, and find your dream home in this vibrant and welcoming country.

CHAPTER TWENTY: Utilities and Communication Services

Setting up your utilities and communication services is one of the first things you'll need to do after finding a place to live in Malaysia. Fortunately, the process is generally straightforward, with a range of providers and options to choose from. This chapter will guide you through the essential steps for setting up your electricity, water, gas, internet, and mobile phone services, ensuring you have a comfortable and connected life in your new Malaysian home.

Electricity: Powering Your Malaysian Life

Tenaga Nasional Berhad (TNB), commonly known as TNB, is the primary electricity provider in Peninsular Malaysia. In East Malaysia (Sabah and Sarawak), electricity services are provided by Sabah Electricity Sdn Bhd (SESB) in Sabah and Sarawak Energy Berhad (SEB) in Sarawak.

Setting Up Your Electricity Account: A Simple Process

To set up your electricity account, you'll need to visit the nearest TNB (or SESB/SEB in East Malaysia) office and provide the following documents:

- **Passport:** Your passport, with a valid visa.

- **Tenancy Agreement or Property Ownership Documents:** Proof of your residency, such as a tenancy agreement or a copy of your property title.

- **Security Deposit:** A refundable security deposit, which varies depending on the type of property and estimated electricity consumption.

You'll need to fill out an application form, provide your signature, and pay the security deposit. Once your application is processed, TNB (or SESB/SEB) will activate your electricity supply, usually within a few working days.

Understanding Electricity Tariffs: How You're Billed

Electricity tariffs in Malaysia are regulated by the Energy Commission. The tariffs are based on a tiered system, where the rate per unit (kWh) increases as your electricity consumption increases. This encourages energy conservation and makes electricity more affordable for those with lower consumption levels.

TNB (or SESB/SEB) will send you a monthly electricity bill, which you can pay online, at TNB offices, or through authorized payment channels, such as banks or convenience stores.

Tips for Managing Your Electricity Consumption

Here are some tips for managing your electricity consumption and reducing your electricity bills:

- **Use Energy-Efficient Appliances:** Choose appliances with high energy efficiency ratings, such as refrigerators, washing machines, and air conditioners.

- **Turn Off Lights and Appliances When Not in Use:** Develop a habit of switching off lights and appliances when you leave a room or when they are not in use.

- **Optimize Air Conditioner Use:** Set your air conditioner to a comfortable temperature, typically around 24-25 degrees Celsius, and use fans to circulate air.

- **Utilize Natural Light:** Open curtains and blinds during the day to maximize natural light and reduce the need for artificial lighting.

- **Unplug Chargers and Devices:** Even when not in use, chargers and electronic devices plugged into outlets can continue to draw power. Unplug them when not charging or using them.

Water: Staying Hydrated and Keeping Things Flowing

Water supply services in Malaysia are managed by state-owned water companies. In Peninsular Malaysia, each state has its own water supply company, such as Syarikat Bekalan Air Selangor Sdn Bhd (SYABAS) in Selangor and Perbadanan Bekalan Air Pulau Pinang Sdn Bhd (PBAPP) in Penang. In East Malaysia, water supply services are provided by the Sabah Water Department in Sabah and the Kuching Water Board in Sarawak.

Setting Up Your Water Account: Easy as a Turn of the Tap

The process for setting up a water account is similar to setting up an electricity account. You'll need to visit the nearest office of your state's water supply company and provide the following documents:

- **Passport:** Your passport, with a valid visa.

- **Tenancy Agreement or Property Ownership Documents:** Proof of your residency.

- **Security Deposit:** A refundable security deposit, which varies depending on the type of property and estimated water consumption.

You'll need to complete an application form, provide your signature, and pay the security deposit. The water supply company will then activate your water supply.

Water Tariffs: Paying for What You Use

Water tariffs in Malaysia are also regulated by the government, with rates varying by state and consumption levels. You'll receive a monthly water bill, which you can pay online, at the water company's offices, or through authorized payment channels.

Tips for Conserving Water: Being Water-Wise

Water conservation is essential, particularly in a tropical country like Malaysia. Here are some tips for reducing your water consumption:

- **Fix Leaks Promptly:** Repair any leaks in faucets, pipes, or toilets to prevent water wastage.

- **Use Water-Efficient Fixtures:** Install water-efficient showerheads, faucets, and toilets.

- **Take Shorter Showers:** Limit your shower time to save water.

- **Turn Off the Tap When Not in Use:** Don't leave the tap running while brushing your teeth, washing dishes, or shaving.

- **Water Your Plants Wisely:** Water your plants during the cooler hours of the day to reduce evaporation and use a watering can instead of a hose.

Gas: Fueling Your Kitchen

Gas supply in Malaysia is primarily provided by Gas Malaysia Berhad in Peninsular Malaysia. In East Malaysia, gas supply is provided by Sabah Energy Corporation (SEC) in Sabah and Sarawak Gas Distribution Sdn Bhd in Sarawak.

Types of Gas Supply: Piped Gas vs. LPG Cylinders

- **Piped Gas:** In some urban areas, piped gas is available, providing a continuous supply of natural gas to your home. Piped gas is generally more convenient and safer than LPG cylinders.

- **LPG Cylinders:** LPG (liquefied petroleum gas) cylinders are a common alternative to piped gas, particularly in areas where piped gas is not available. LPG cylinders are delivered to your home and connected to your gas appliances.

Setting Up Your Gas Account: Connecting the Flow

If you opt for piped gas, you'll need to contact Gas Malaysia Berhad (or SEC/Sarawak Gas Distribution in East Malaysia) to set up an account. You'll need to provide your property details and sign a supply agreement. Gas Malaysia will then install a gas meter at your property and activate your gas supply.

For LPG cylinders, you can contact authorized LPG distributors to arrange for cylinder deliveries and connections.

Gas Tariffs: Paying for Your Fuel

Gas tariffs in Malaysia are regulated by the government. For piped gas, you'll receive a monthly bill based on your gas consumption. For LPG cylinders, you'll pay for each cylinder upon delivery.

Gas Safety Tips: Keeping Things Safe and Secure

Gas safety is crucial, whether you're using piped gas or LPG cylinders. Here are some essential safety tips:

- **Regular Inspections:** Have your gas appliances and piping system regularly inspected by a qualified technician to ensure they are in good working order and to detect any potential leaks.

- **Ventilation:** Ensure your kitchen and other areas where gas appliances are used are well-ventilated to prevent the build-up of gas fumes.

- **Gas Leak Detection:** Be aware of the signs of a gas leak, such as a rotten egg smell, hissing sound, or white cloud near gas appliances. If you suspect a gas leak, turn off the gas supply at the main valve, open windows for ventilation, and contact Gas Malaysia (or SEC/Sarawak Gas Distribution) immediately.

- **LPG Cylinder Safety:** Store LPG cylinders in a well-ventilated area, away from heat sources and flammable materials. Handle cylinders with care to avoid damage or leaks.

Internet: Staying Connected in the Digital Age

Staying connected is essential in today's digital world, and Malaysia offers reliable and relatively affordable internet services, with a range of providers and plans to choose from.

Choosing an Internet Service Provider (ISP)

When selecting an ISP, consider the following factors:

- **Coverage:** Check if the ISP offers coverage in your area.

- **Speed and Data Allowance:** Choose a plan with a speed and data allowance that meets your needs, whether you're a casual internet user or a heavy streamer or gamer.

- **Price:** Compare prices from different ISPs to find a plan that fits your budget.

- **Customer Service:** Read online reviews and ask for recommendations from other expats to gauge the ISP's customer service reputation.

Types of Internet Connections: Fiber Optic vs. DSL

- **Fiber Optic:** Fiber optic internet offers the fastest speeds and most reliable connection, with download and upload speeds of up to 1 Gbps (gigabits per second). Fiber optic infrastructure is expanding rapidly in Malaysia, making it increasingly available in urban and suburban areas.

- **DSL (Digital Subscriber Line):** DSL internet uses existing telephone lines to provide internet access. DSL speeds are generally slower than fiber optic, but it's often a more affordable option, particularly in areas where fiber optic is not yet available.

Setting Up Your Internet Connection: Getting Online

To set up your internet connection, contact your chosen ISP and select a plan that meets your needs. You'll need to provide your property details and sign a service agreement. The ISP will then schedule an installation appointment, typically within a few working days.

During the installation, a technician will install a modem and router at your property and configure your internet connection. Once the installation is complete, you'll be able to connect your devices and enjoy high-speed internet access.

Tips for Optimizing Your Internet Experience

Here are some tips for optimizing your internet experience:

- **Choose the Right Router:** Invest in a high-quality router that supports the latest Wi-Fi standards for optimal speed and coverage.

- **Secure Your Wi-Fi Network:** Set up a strong password for your Wi-Fi network to prevent unauthorized access and protect your data.

- **Use a VPN (Virtual Private Network):** A VPN encrypts your internet traffic, protecting your privacy and security, especially when using public Wi-Fi networks.

- **Manage Data Usage:** Monitor your data usage to avoid exceeding your plan's allowance and incurring additional charges.

Mobile Phones: Staying Connected on the Go

Mobile phone services in Malaysia are provided by several major telecommunications companies, including Celcom, Digi, Maxis, and U Mobile.

Choosing a Mobile Phone Plan: Prepaid vs. Postpaid

- **Prepaid Plans:** Prepaid plans offer flexibility, allowing you to top up your credit as needed. They are a good option for those who don't use their phones frequently or prefer to have more control over their spending.

- **Postpaid Plans:** Postpaid plans offer a monthly allowance of calls, data, and SMS, with a fixed monthly bill. They are often more cost-effective for those who use their phones heavily.

Setting Up Your Mobile Phone Service: Staying in Touch

To set up your mobile phone service, you can visit a store of your chosen telecommunications company, an authorized dealer, or purchase a SIM card online. You'll need to provide your passport and visa details for registration.

Once you have a SIM card, you can choose a prepaid or postpaid plan that suits your needs. You can easily top up your prepaid credit at convenience stores, online, or through mobile banking apps.

Mobile Data and Roaming: Staying Connected Anywhere

Most mobile phone plans in Malaysia include data allowances, allowing you to access the internet on your phone. If you're traveling outside of Malaysia, check with your telecommunications company about roaming charges and data packages to avoid unexpected bills.

Mobile Apps: Enhancing Your Mobile Experience

Malaysia has a thriving mobile app ecosystem, with apps for everything from ride-hailing and food delivery to online shopping and entertainment. Download popular apps like Grab, Foodpanda, Shopee, and Netflix to enhance your mobile experience.

Staying Connected: A Seamless Transition

Setting up your utilities and communication services is an essential step in settling into your new life in Malaysia. With a range of providers, plans, and options to choose from, you can easily find services that meet your needs and budget. By following the steps outlined in this chapter, you can ensure a smooth transition, stay connected, and enjoy a comfortable and convenient life in your new Malaysian home.

CHAPTER TWENTY-ONE: Domestic Help and Daily Life Essentials

Moving to a new country always involves a period of adjustment as you familiarize yourself with new surroundings, customs, and ways of life. In Malaysia, where the cost of living is relatively affordable, many expats find that hiring domestic help can significantly ease the transition and free up valuable time to focus on work, family, and exploring your new home. This chapter will delve into the practical aspects of hiring domestic help in Malaysia, covering the types of services available, legal considerations, hiring processes, and essential tips for managing a harmonious employer-employee relationship. We'll also explore other daily life essentials, such as grocery shopping, laundry services, and other conveniences that can simplify your life in Malaysia.

Domestic Help in Malaysia: A Common Practice

Hiring domestic help is a common practice in Malaysia, both among local families and expats. The relatively low cost of labor and the availability of skilled and experienced domestic helpers make it a viable option for many households. Domestic helpers can assist with a range of tasks, freeing up your time and easing the burden of daily chores.

Types of Domestic Help Services

Domestic helpers in Malaysia can provide a variety of services, tailored to your specific needs and preferences. Some common types of domestic help include:

- **Live-In Maids:** Live-in maids reside in your home and provide full-time assistance with household chores, such as cleaning, cooking, laundry, ironing, and childcare.

- **Live-Out Maids:** Live-out maids do not reside in your home and typically work for a set number of hours per day or week. They can assist with similar tasks as live-in maids, but they have their own living arrangements.

- **Part-Time Cleaners:** Part-time cleaners typically work for a few hours per week, focusing primarily on cleaning tasks, such as dusting, vacuuming, mopping, and cleaning bathrooms and kitchens.

- **Cooks:** If you prefer to have someone prepare your meals, you can hire a cook who specializes in Malaysian cuisine, international cuisine, or specific dietary requirements.

- **Nannies or Babysitters:** For families with young children, nannies or babysitters can provide childcare assistance, either on a full-time or part-time basis.

- **Gardeners:** If you have a garden, you can hire a gardener to maintain your lawn, trim hedges, and care for your plants.

Legal Considerations: Hiring Domestic Help Legally and Ethically

Hiring domestic help in Malaysia is subject to legal regulations and ethical considerations. It's crucial to comply with these regulations to ensure a fair and respectful working relationship.

Employment Act 1955: Protecting Workers' Rights

The Employment Act 1955 outlines the basic rights and protections for employees in Malaysia, including domestic helpers. Key provisions of the Act include:

- **Minimum Wage:** Domestic helpers are entitled to a minimum wage, which is set by the government and varies by region.

- **Working Hours:** The Act limits the number of working hours per day and week, and domestic helpers are entitled to rest days and annual leave.

- **Overtime Pay:** Domestic helpers are entitled to overtime pay for working beyond the stipulated working hours.

- **Public Holidays:** Domestic helpers are entitled to paid public holidays.

- **Termination of Employment:** The Act outlines procedures for terminating employment, including notice periods and termination benefits.

Immigration Regulations: Hiring Foreign Domestic Helpers

Most domestic helpers in Malaysia are foreign nationals, primarily from Indonesia, the Philippines, and other Southeast Asian countries. Hiring a foreign domestic helper requires adhering to immigration regulations and obtaining the necessary work permits.

The process typically involves:

1. **Employer Application:** As the employer, you'll need to submit an application to the Immigration Department of Malaysia for a work permit for your domestic helper.

2. **Supporting Documents:** You'll need to provide supporting documents, such as your passport, visa, employment contract, and proof of your ability to provide accommodation and financial support for the domestic helper.

3. **Security Bond:** You may be required to post a security bond with the Immigration Department, which is refundable upon the domestic helper's departure from Malaysia.

4. **Medical Examination:** The domestic helper will need to undergo a medical examination to ensure they are fit to work in Malaysia.

5. **Visa Issuance:** Once the application is approved, the domestic helper will be issued a visa allowing them to work in Malaysia.

Hiring Process: Finding the Right Domestic Helper

Finding a reliable and trustworthy domestic helper requires careful planning and a thorough hiring process. Here are some steps to consider:

1. Determine Your Needs:

Clearly define the tasks and responsibilities you expect from a domestic helper. Consider the number of hours you require assistance, the specific tasks you need help with (cleaning, cooking, childcare, etc.), and any specific skills or experience you require.

2. Explore Different Options:

You can find domestic helpers through various channels:

- **Maid Agencies:** Maid agencies specialize in recruiting and placing domestic helpers. They can screen candidates, handle paperwork, and facilitate the immigration process.

- **Online Platforms:** Websites and social media groups dedicated to domestic help services offer listings of available helpers, allowing you to connect with them directly.

- **Word-of-Mouth Referrals:** Ask friends, colleagues, or neighbors for recommendations on reliable domestic helpers.

3. Interview Candidates:

Once you have a shortlist of potential candidates, conduct interviews to assess their suitability. Prepare a list of questions to ask about their experience, skills, availability, and expectations. Observe their communication skills, attitude, and overall demeanor.

4. Check References:

Request references from previous employers and verify their authenticity. Speaking with previous employers can provide valuable insights into the candidate's work ethic, reliability, and character.

5. Background Check (Optional):

You can conduct a background check on the candidate, particularly if you are hiring someone to work with children or handle sensitive information.

6. Negotiate Terms and Conditions:

Once you have selected a candidate, clearly discuss the terms and conditions of employment, including salary, working hours, rest days, annual leave, and other benefits. Ensure you are both in agreement and document these terms in a written employment contract.

7. Sign an Employment Contract:

Both you and the domestic helper should sign a written employment contract that outlines the terms and conditions of employment. This contract serves as a legal document and helps prevent misunderstandings or disputes.

Managing Employer-Employee Relations: Building a Harmonious Household

Hiring a domestic helper involves welcoming someone into your home and building a working relationship that is both respectful and efficient. Here are some tips for managing a harmonious employer-employee relationship:

1. Clear Communication:

Establish clear communication from the outset, outlining your expectations, house rules, and any specific preferences. Encourage open communication and provide opportunities for the domestic helper to ask questions or voice concerns.

2. Respectful Treatment:

Treat your domestic helper with respect and dignity, acknowledging their contributions and valuing their work. Avoid raising your voice, making disparaging remarks, or engaging in any form of abuse or exploitation.

3. Fair Compensation:

Pay your domestic helper the agreed-upon salary on time, and ensure they are receiving the minimum wage and other benefits as stipulated by law.

4. Provide Comfortable Accommodation:

If you are hiring a live-in maid, provide comfortable and private accommodation. Ensure they have access to basic amenities, such as a bed, wardrobe, and bathroom facilities.

5. Respect Rest Days and Leave:

Allow your domestic helper to take their entitled rest days and annual leave. Encourage them to take breaks and ensure they have time for personal errands or relaxation.

6. Address Concerns Promptly:

Address any concerns or issues promptly and professionally. Encourage open dialogue and seek solutions that are fair and mutually acceptable.

7. Cultural Sensitivity:

Be mindful of cultural differences and sensitivities, particularly if your domestic helper is from a different country or cultural background. Respect their customs, traditions, and beliefs.

Daily Life Essentials: Simplifying Your Routine

Beyond domestic help, Malaysia offers a range of services and conveniences that can simplify your daily life, freeing up time to focus on other priorities.

Grocery Shopping: From Markets to Online Delivery

Malaysia offers a variety of options for grocery shopping, from bustling local markets to modern supermarkets and convenient online delivery services.

- **Local Markets (Pasar):** Local markets are a vibrant part of Malaysian life, offering fresh produce, seafood, meats, spices, and other ingredients, often at lower prices than supermarkets. Bargaining is a common practice at local markets.

- **Supermarkets:** Supermarkets, such as AEON, Tesco, Giant, and Village Grocer, offer a wide range of groceries, household essentials, and imported products. Supermarkets typically accept credit cards and offer loyalty programs.

- **Online Grocery Delivery:** Online platforms like HappyFresh, GrabMart, and Tesco Online offer the convenience of ordering groceries online and having them delivered to your doorstep.

Laundry Services: Keeping Things Clean and Fresh

- **Self-Service Laundromats (Dobi):** Self-service laundromats are widely available, particularly in urban areas. They offer coin-operated washing machines and dryers, allowing you to do your laundry conveniently.

- **Laundry Shops:** Laundry shops provide professional laundry and dry-cleaning services, offering wash-and-fold, ironing, and dry-cleaning for various types of clothing.

- **Home Delivery Laundry Services:** Some laundry shops offer pick-up and delivery services, collecting your laundry from your home and delivering it back to you clean and folded.

Other Daily Life Conveniences: Simplifying Errands

Malaysia offers a range of other services that can simplify your daily life:

- **Food Delivery:** Food delivery apps like GrabFood and Foodpanda allow you to order meals from a wide variety of restaurants and have them delivered to your home or office.

- **Ride-Hailing Services:** Ride-hailing services like Grab provide convenient and affordable transportation, allowing you to book rides from your smartphone.

- **Online Shopping:** E-commerce platforms like Shopee and Lazada offer a vast array of products, from electronics and fashion to groceries and homeware, with the convenience of online shopping and home delivery.

- **Bill Payment Services:** You can pay your utility bills, phone bills, and other bills online, through mobile banking apps, or at convenience stores.

Embracing the Convenience: A More Balanced Life

Hiring domestic help and utilizing the various services and conveniences available in Malaysia can significantly simplify your daily life, freeing up valuable time to focus on work, family, and exploring your new home. By understanding the legal considerations, hiring processes, and tips for managing employer-employee relations, you can ensure a fair and respectful working relationship with your domestic helper. Embracing these conveniences can contribute to a more balanced and enjoyable life in Malaysia.

CHAPTER TWENTY-TWO: Legal Matters: Understanding the Malaysian Legal System

Moving to a new country requires familiarizing yourself with its legal system, even if you have no intention of getting into any trouble. Ignorance of the law is no excuse anywhere in the world and Malaysia is no different in this respect. This chapter provides expats with a general overview of the legal system in Malaysia, highlighting key aspects that are relevant to daily life, business operations, and personal conduct. We'll explore the sources of law, the court structure, common legal issues expats may encounter, and resources for seeking legal assistance.

Sources of Malaysian Law: A Blend of Traditions

The Malaysian legal system is a fascinating blend of common law, Islamic law, and customary law, reflecting the country's historical influences and diverse cultural heritage. Understanding the sources of law is essential for comprehending the legal framework and how it applies to various aspects of life in Malaysia.

Common Law: The Legacy of British Rule

The foundation of the Malaysian legal system is rooted in common law, inherited from British colonial rule. Common law is based on judicial precedents, meaning that court decisions in previous cases serve as binding authority for future cases with similar facts.

The principles of common law, such as the rule of law, due process, and the separation of powers, form the bedrock of the Malaysian legal system, ensuring fairness, consistency, and the protection of individual rights.

Islamic Law (Sharia): Guiding Principles for Muslims

Islamic law, known as Sharia, plays a significant role in the lives of Muslims in Malaysia, governing matters of personal conduct, family law, and inheritance. Sharia courts have jurisdiction over Muslims in these matters, applying Islamic legal principles derived from the Quran and the Sunnah (teachings and practices of Prophet Muhammad).

Customary Law: Traditional Practices of Indigenous Communities

Customary law, reflecting the traditional practices and beliefs of indigenous communities, also holds a place in the Malaysian legal system, particularly in matters related to land ownership, inheritance, and traditional dispute resolution mechanisms within these communities.

Court Structure: A Hierarchy of Justice

The Malaysian court system is structured hierarchically, with different levels of courts handling various types of cases.

Court Level	Jurisdiction
Magistrate's Court	Handles minor criminal offenses and civil cases involving limited monetary amounts.
Sessions Court	Handles more serious criminal offenses and civil cases involving larger monetary amounts.
High Court	Has original jurisdiction over all criminal and civil cases, including those involving constitutional matters. It also hears appeals from lower courts.
Court of Appeal	Hears appeals from the High Court.
Federal Court	The highest court in Malaysia, hearing appeals from the Court of Appeal and having original jurisdiction over certain constitutional matters.

Common Legal Issues: Navigating Potential Challenges

Expats in Malaysia may encounter various legal issues related to employment, immigration, property, and personal conduct. Here are some common areas to be aware of:

Employment Law: Protecting Your Rights as an Employee

The Employment Act 1955 governs employment relationships in Malaysia, outlining the rights and obligations of both employers and employees. Key provisions of the Act include:

- **Minimum Wage:** Employees are entitled to a minimum wage, which is set by the government and varies by region.

- **Working Hours:** The Act limits the number of working hours per day and week, and employees are entitled to rest days and annual leave.

- **Overtime Pay:** Employees are entitled to overtime pay for working beyond the stipulated working hours.

- **Public Holidays:** Employees are entitled to paid public holidays.

- **Termination of Employment:** The Act outlines procedures for terminating employment, including notice periods and termination benefits.

If you encounter any issues related to your employment, such as unfair dismissal, unpaid wages, or breach of contract, you can seek legal assistance from the Industrial Relations Department or the Labour Court.

Immigration Law: Staying Legally Compliant

Immigration regulations in Malaysia are strict, and it's crucial for expats to ensure they have the necessary visas and work permits to reside and work in the country legally. Overstaying your visa or working without a valid permit can result in fines, imprisonment, or deportation.

Always ensure your visa is up-to-date, apply for extensions or renewals as needed, and comply with immigration regulations. If you encounter any issues related to immigration, seek legal assistance from an immigration lawyer or consult the Immigration Department of Malaysia.

Property Law: Understanding Ownership and Transactions

Property law in Malaysia governs matters related to property ownership, purchase, sale, leasing, and inheritance. If you are considering buying or renting property, it's essential to understand your rights and obligations, ensure the property has clear title, and engage a lawyer to review any contracts or agreements.

Common issues related to property law include:

- **Land Ownership:** Foreigners are generally allowed to purchase property in Malaysia, but there may be restrictions on certain types of properties or locations.

- **Strata Title:** Apartments and condominiums typically have strata titles, which grant individual ownership of the unit and shared ownership of common areas. Understand the rules and regulations governing strata properties.

- **Lease Agreements:** Review lease agreements carefully before signing, ensuring you understand the terms and conditions, including the rental price, lease duration, and responsibilities for maintenance and repairs.

- **Property Disputes:** If you encounter any disputes with your landlord, tenant, or neighbor related to property matters, seek legal assistance from a property lawyer or the relevant authorities.

Personal Conduct: Respecting Local Laws and Customs

Malaysia has laws and regulations governing personal conduct, and it's important for expats to be aware of these to avoid potential legal issues or cultural misunderstandings. Here are some key areas to be mindful of:

- **Drug Offenses:** Drug offenses are taken very seriously in Malaysia, with severe penalties, including lengthy prison sentences or even the death penalty for trafficking or possession of certain drugs.

- **Alcohol Consumption:** While alcohol consumption is legal in Malaysia, there are restrictions on its sale and consumption in certain areas, particularly in Muslim-majority states. Be respectful of local customs and regulations.

- **Public Decency:** Public displays of affection, such as kissing or hugging, are generally frowned upon in Malaysia, particularly in conservative areas. Dress modestly, especially when visiting religious sites or attending formal events.

- **Gambling:** Gambling is illegal in Malaysia, except for licensed casinos in certain locations.

- **Defamation:** Making false or defamatory statements about someone can be a legal offense in Malaysia.

Seeking Legal Assistance: Finding the Right Support

If you require legal assistance in Malaysia, there are various resources available:

- **Lawyers:** Engage a lawyer who specializes in the relevant area of law, such as employment law, immigration law, or property law. The Malaysian Bar Council can provide a list of registered lawyers.

- **Embassy or Consulate:** Your home country's embassy or consulate in Malaysia may be able to provide a list of lawyers or legal aid organizations.

- **Legal Aid Organizations:** Non-governmental organizations, such as the Legal Aid Centre, provide free or low-cost legal assistance to those who cannot afford legal representation.

Understanding the Legal Landscape: A Key to a Smooth Experience

Understanding the legal system in Malaysia is essential for expats to navigate daily life, conduct business, and avoid potential legal issues. By familiarizing yourself with the sources of law, the court structure, common legal areas, and resources for seeking legal assistance, you can ensure a smoother and more secure experience in your new Malaysian home.

CHAPTER TWENTY-THREE: Retirement in Malaysia: A Peaceful and Affordable Option

Retirement is a time for relaxation, exploration, and pursuing passions that may have been put on hold during your working years. For many people, the idea of retiring abroad holds a certain allure, the promise of a new adventure, a change of scenery, and a chance to experience a different way of life. Malaysia, with its warm tropical climate, diverse culture, affordable cost of living, and welcoming environment, has emerged as a popular destination for retirees seeking a peaceful and fulfilling retirement.

This chapter will explore the allure of retiring in Malaysia, delving into the benefits, the practical considerations, the visa options specifically designed for retirees, the best places to retire, and the lifestyle you can expect in this Southeast Asian paradise.

The Allure of Malaysia: Why Retire Here?

Malaysia offers a compelling combination of factors that make it an attractive retirement destination:

Affordable Cost of Living: Stretching Your Retirement Savings

One of the most significant advantages of retiring in Malaysia is the relatively low cost of living compared to many Western countries. Your retirement savings can go much further in Malaysia, allowing you to enjoy a comfortable lifestyle without breaking the bank.

Housing, food, transportation, healthcare, and entertainment are all generally affordable in Malaysia. You can find comfortable accommodations, savor delicious meals, explore the country, and enjoy a variety of activities without straining your budget.

Warm Tropical Climate: Year-Round Sunshine

Malaysia's tropical climate, with warm temperatures and sunshine year-round, is a major draw for retirees seeking to escape the cold winters or unpredictable weather of their home countries. Enjoy outdoor activities, relax on beautiful beaches, or explore the lush rainforests without having to worry about snow, ice, or freezing temperatures.

Diverse Culture and Heritage: A Tapestry of Experiences

Malaysia's multicultural society, with its blend of Malay, Chinese, Indian, and indigenous influences, creates a rich and vibrant cultural tapestry. Immerse yourself in a world of diverse traditions, festivals, cuisines, languages, and arts, experiencing a kaleidoscope of cultural encounters that will enrich your retirement years.

Friendly and Welcoming People: A Sense of Community

Malaysians are generally known for their warm hospitality and welcoming nature. You'll likely experience a sense of community and belonging, making it easier to adjust to your new surroundings and build new friendships.

English Proficiency: Easing Communication

English is widely spoken in Malaysia, particularly in urban areas and business settings. This makes it relatively easy for expats to communicate, navigate daily life, and access services without facing significant language barriers.

Modern Infrastructure and Amenities: Convenient Living

Malaysia boasts modern infrastructure and amenities, making daily life convenient and comfortable. From well-maintained roads and efficient public transportation to world-class shopping malls, healthcare facilities, and reliable internet connectivity, you'll find everything you need for a comfortable and fulfilling retirement.

Healthcare: Quality and Affordable Medical Services

Malaysia's healthcare system is often lauded for its quality, affordability, and efficiency. The country offers both public and private healthcare options, with a range of hospitals, clinics, and specialized medical professionals. Retirees can access affordable and high-quality healthcare, ensuring their well-being in their retirement years.

Travel Opportunities: Exploring Southeast Asia and Beyond

Malaysia's strategic location in the heart of Southeast Asia makes it an ideal base for exploring the region and beyond. With affordable flights, convenient visa policies, and a diverse range of destinations within easy reach, you can embark on exciting adventures, discover new cultures, and create unforgettable travel memories during your retirement.

Malaysia My Second Home (MM2H) Program: A Visa for Retirees

The Malaysia My Second Home (MM2H) program is a long-term visa specifically designed for foreigners who wish to reside in Malaysia for an extended period, typically 10 years, with the option for renewal. This program is particularly popular among retirees seeking a peaceful and affordable retirement destination.

Eligibility Criteria: Meeting the Requirements

To qualify for the MM2H program, you must meet certain financial and age requirements:

- **Age:** Applicants must be at least 50 years old (or 40 years old for those applying with dependents).

- **Financial Requirements:** Applicants must prove they have sufficient financial means to support themselves during their stay in Malaysia. This can be demonstrated through:

    - **Fixed Deposit:** Applicants must maintain a fixed deposit of a specified amount in a Malaysian bank. The amount varies depending on your age and nationality.

    - **Offshore Income:** Applicants must have a minimum monthly offshore income, the amount of which varies depending on your age and nationality.

Benefits of the MM2H Program:

- **Long-Term Visa:** Successful applicants are granted a 10-year visa, which is renewable thereafter.

- **Multiple Entry:** The visa allows multiple entries and exits from Malaysia, giving you the flexibility to travel freely.

- **Dependent Visa:** Spouses, children under 21 years old, and parents over 60 years old can be included in the visa application.

- **Property Ownership:** MM2H visa holders are allowed to purchase property in Malaysia, subject to certain minimum purchase price requirements, which vary by state.

- **Car Ownership:** MM2H visa holders can purchase and own cars in Malaysia.

- **Tax Benefits:** MM2H visa holders may be eligible for tax exemptions on certain income sources.

Application Process: Securing Your MM2H Visa

The MM2H application process involves several steps:

1. **Submitting an Application:** Applicants can submit their applications online or through a Malaysian embassy or consulate in their home country.

2. **Providing Supporting Documents:** Applicants must provide supporting documents, such as passport copies, financial statements, and proof of age.

3. **Attending an Interview (if required):** Shortlisted applicants may be required to attend an interview at a Malaysian embassy or consulate.

4. **Paying the Application Fee:** The MM2H application fee is non-refundable.

5. **Receiving a Conditional Approval Letter:** If the application is successful, applicants will receive a conditional approval letter.

6. **Opening a Fixed Deposit Account:** Applicants must open a fixed deposit account in a Malaysian bank and deposit the required amount.

7. **Obtaining a Visa:** Upon fulfillment of the financial requirements, applicants will be granted the MM2H visa.

Best Places to Retire in Malaysia: Finding Your Perfect Haven

Malaysia offers a diverse range of retirement destinations, each with its own unique charm, lifestyle, and appeal. The best place for you to retire will depend on your personal preferences, budget, and desired lifestyle.

Here are some of the most popular retirement destinations in Malaysia:

Penang: Island Living with Colonial Charm

Penang, an island state off the northwest coast of Peninsular Malaysia, is renowned for its colonial heritage, vibrant street art scene, and delectable street food. It offers a more relaxed pace of life compared to Kuala Lumpur, with a unique blend of old-world charm and modern amenities.

Here's why Penang is a popular retirement destination:

- **Affordable Cost of Living:** Penang generally offers a lower cost of living compared to Kuala Lumpur, making it more affordable for retirees.

- **Cultural Diversity:** Penang is a melting pot of cultures, with a harmonious blend of Malay, Chinese, Indian, and Peranakan influences. Explore historical landmarks, vibrant markets, and diverse culinary offerings.

- **Nature and Beaches:** Penang boasts beautiful beaches, lush hills, and national parks, offering opportunities for outdoor recreation, relaxation, and nature exploration.

- **Healthcare:** Penang has well-equipped hospitals and clinics, providing access to quality healthcare services.

Popular Retirement Spots in Penang:

- **George Town:** A UNESCO World Heritage City, George Town offers a captivating blend of historical architecture, street art, and a thriving culinary scene.

- **Batu Ferringhi:** A popular beach destination on the north coast of Penang, offering a range of resorts, hotels, restaurants, and watersports activities.

- **Tanjung Bungah:** A coastal suburb with a mix of high-rise condominiums, landed properties, and seafront views, offering a more tranquil environment.

Kuala Lumpur: The Cosmopolitan Hub

Kuala Lumpur, the vibrant capital city, is a dynamic metropolis that offers a wide range of amenities, entertainment options, and a cosmopolitan lifestyle. While the cost of living in Kuala Lumpur is generally higher than in other parts of Malaysia, it's still relatively affordable compared to many major cities worldwide.

Here's why Kuala Lumpur might appeal to some retirees:

- **Modern Infrastructure:** Kuala Lumpur boasts excellent infrastructure, including efficient public transportation, well-maintained roads, and modern amenities.

- **Entertainment and Shopping:** The city offers a plethora of entertainment and shopping options, from world-class cinemas and live music venues to sprawling shopping malls and bustling street markets.

- **Healthcare:** Kuala Lumpur has top-notch hospitals and clinics, providing access to specialized medical care and treatments.

- **International Community:** The city has a large expat community, making it easier to connect with people from similar backgrounds and build a social circle.

Popular Retirement Spots in Kuala Lumpur:

- **Mont Kiara:** A popular expat enclave known for its upscale condominiums, international schools, and family-friendly atmosphere.

- **Bangsar:** A vibrant suburb with a bohemian vibe, offering trendy cafes, bars, restaurants, and independent boutiques.

- **Taman Tun Dr Ismail (TTDI):** A leafy suburb with a more laid-back feel, offering spacious landed properties and a good selection of local eateries and shops.

Langkawi: Island Paradise with Duty-Free Shopping

Langkawi, an archipelago of 99 islands off the northwest coast of Peninsular Malaysia, is a tropical paradise known for its beautiful beaches, lush rainforests, duty-free shopping, and laid-back island lifestyle.

Here's why Langkawi might appeal to retirees:

- **Natural Beauty:** Langkawi boasts pristine beaches, crystal-clear waters, lush rainforests, and waterfalls, offering opportunities for relaxation, nature exploration, and outdoor activities.

- **Duty-Free Shopping:** Langkawi is a duty-free zone, making it an attractive destination for shopping, particularly for alcohol, tobacco, and luxury goods.

- **Affordable Living:** The cost of living in Langkawi is generally lower than in major cities like Kuala Lumpur or Penang.

- **Relaxed Atmosphere:** Langkawi offers a tranquil and laid-back island lifestyle, a perfect escape from the hustle and bustle of city life.

Popular Retirement Spots in Langkawi:

- **Pantai Cenang:** The most popular beach area in Langkawi, offering a variety of hotels, restaurants, bars, and watersports activities.

- **Pantai Tengah:** A more tranquil beach area, known for its resorts and spas, offering a relaxing getaway.

- **Kuah Town:** The main town in Langkawi, offering a mix of shops, restaurants, and local markets.

Malacca: Historical Charm and Coastal Living

Malacca, a UNESCO World Heritage City on the southwestern coast of Peninsular Malaysia, is steeped in history and offers a unique blend of cultural heritage, coastal living, and a relaxed atmosphere.

Here's why Malacca might appeal to retirees:

- **Historical Significance:** Malacca's rich history, influenced by Malay, Portuguese, Dutch, and British rule, is reflected in its colonial architecture, ancient temples, and cultural landmarks. Explore historical sites, museums, and heritage trails.

- **Coastal Lifestyle:** Malacca offers a coastal lifestyle, with access to beaches, seafood restaurants, and waterfront promenades.

- **Affordable Living:** The cost of living in Malacca is generally lower than in major cities, making it more affordable for retirees.

Popular Retirement Spots in Malacca:

- **Jonker Street:** A historic street lined with traditional shophouses, antique shops, art galleries, and restaurants, offering a glimpse into Malacca's past.

- **Portuguese Settlement:** A community of descendants of Portuguese colonists, with colorful houses, traditional cuisine, and a unique cultural heritage.

- **Klebang Beach:** A popular beach area known for its coconut shake, a refreshing local drink.

Ipoh: A City of Heritage and Gastronomy

Ipoh, the capital city of Perak state in Peninsular Malaysia, is known for its limestone caves, colonial architecture, and delectable cuisine. It offers a more laid-back and affordable alternative to Kuala Lumpur.

Here's why Ipoh might appeal to retirees:

- **Historical Heritage:** Ipoh's history is reflected in its colonial-era buildings, such as the Ipoh Railway Station and the Birch Memorial Clock Tower. Explore historical sites, museums, and heritage trails.

- **Cave Temples:** Ipoh is surrounded by limestone hills, home to numerous cave temples, including the Kek Lok Tong Cave Temple and the Sam Poh Tong Cave Temple.

- **Gastronomy:** Ipoh is renowned for its cuisine, particularly its white coffee, bean sprouts chicken, and caramel custard.

Popular Retirement Spots in Ipoh:

- **Ipoh Old Town:** The historical heart of Ipoh, with its colonial-era buildings, street art, and charming cafes.

- **Tambun:** A suburb known for its hot springs, theme park, and natural attractions, offering a blend of relaxation and entertainment.

- **Meru:** A quiet residential area with a mix of landed properties and apartments, offering a peaceful retreat.

Kota Kinabalu (Sabah): Coastal Living in Borneo

Kota Kinabalu, the capital city of Sabah state in East Malaysia (Borneo), offers a coastal lifestyle, stunning sunsets, and access to nearby islands and national parks.

Here's why Kota Kinabalu might appeal to retirees:

- **Natural Beauty:** Kota Kinabalu is surrounded by stunning natural beauty, including Mount Kinabalu, the Crocker

Range, and the Tunku Abdul Rahman National Park, offering opportunities for hiking, trekking, and nature exploration.

- **Beaches and Islands:** The city has several beaches, and nearby islands, such as Manukan Island and Sapi Island, are easily accessible by boat.

- **Cultural Diversity:** Kota Kinabalu is a multicultural city, with a mix of Malay, Chinese, indigenous, and expat communities.

Popular Retirement Spots in Kota Kinabalu:

- **Likas:** A suburb with a mix of residential areas, beaches, and the Likas Sports Complex.

- **Damai:** A resort area located about 30 minutes from Kota Kinabalu, offering luxury resorts, golf courses, and a beach.

- **Penampang:** A suburb with a mix of residential areas, shops, and restaurants, located about 15 minutes from Kota Kinabalu.

Kuching (Sarawak): The Cat City of Borneo

Kuching, the capital city of Sarawak state in East Malaysia (Borneo), is known as the "Cat City" due to its numerous cat statues and its fondness for felines. The city offers a relaxed atmosphere, a rich cultural heritage, and access to nearby national parks.

Here's why Kuching might appeal to retirees:

- **Cultural Heritage:** Kuching has a rich history, influenced by Malay, Chinese, and indigenous cultures. Explore historical landmarks, museums, and cultural villages.

- **Riverfront Promenade:** The Kuching Waterfront, a scenic promenade along the Sarawak River, is a popular spot for walking, jogging, and enjoying river views.

- **Nature and National Parks:** Kuching is surrounded by national parks, such as Bako National Park and Gunung Gading National Park, offering opportunities for nature exploration and wildlife encounters.

Popular Retirement Spots in Kuching:

- **Kuching City Centre:** The heart of the city, with its historical landmarks, waterfront promenade, and a mix of shops, restaurants, and entertainment options.

- **Damai:** A resort area located about 30 minutes from Kuching, offering luxury resorts, golf courses, and beaches.

- **Santubong:** A coastal area known for its beaches, seafood restaurants, and the Sarawak Cultural Village, a living museum showcasing the cultural heritage of Sarawak's indigenous communities.

Retirement Lifestyle: Embracing the Malaysian Experience

Retiring in Malaysia offers a chance to embrace a new way of life, a blend of relaxation, exploration, cultural immersion, and personal fulfillment.

Activities and Interests: Finding Your Passions

Retirement is a time to pursue passions and interests that may have been put on hold during your working years. Malaysia offers a diverse range of activities and hobbies to keep you engaged and fulfilled.

- **Outdoor Recreation:** Malaysia's natural beauty provides ample opportunities for outdoor recreation, including hiking, trekking, cycling, golfing, fishing, diving, snorkeling, and watersports.

- **Cultural Immersion:** Explore Malaysia's diverse cultural heritage by attending festivals, visiting temples and mosques, learning a new language, or taking cooking classes.

- **Volunteering:** Give back to the community by volunteering your time and skills to local organizations or charities.

- **Social Clubs and Activities:** Join social clubs, hobby groups, or expat organizations to meet like-minded people and pursue your interests.

- **Travel:** Use Malaysia as a base to explore Southeast Asia and beyond, discovering new cultures and destinations.

Cost of Living: Managing Your Budget

While Malaysia generally offers an affordable cost of living, it's essential to plan your budget and manage your expenses wisely. The cost of living will vary depending on your lifestyle, location, and spending habits.

Here are some tips for managing your retirement budget in Malaysia:

- **Track Your Expenses:** Keep track of your spending to identify areas where you can save money.

- **Choose Affordable Housing:** Explore different housing options and choose one that fits your budget and lifestyle. Consider renting instead of buying, particularly if you're unsure about a specific location.

- **Eat Local:** Eating at local hawker centers and food courts is significantly cheaper than dining at restaurants.

- **Utilize Public Transportation:** Public transportation in Malaysia is efficient and affordable. Consider using buses, trains, or ride-hailing services instead of owning a car, particularly in urban areas.

- **Take Advantage of Free Activities:** Malaysia offers plenty of free activities and attractions, such as parks, beaches, and museums.

- **Shop Around for Deals:** Compare prices for groceries, goods, and services to find the best deals.

- **Negotiate Prices:** Bargaining is a common practice in Malaysia, particularly at local markets and street stalls.

- **Live Like a Local:** Embracing the local lifestyle can often lead to a more affordable and authentic experience.

Healthcare: Ensuring Your Well-being

Access to quality healthcare is crucial during retirement. Malaysia's healthcare system offers both public and private options, with a range of hospitals, clinics, and specialized medical professionals.

- **Public Healthcare:** The public healthcare system is heavily subsidized by the government, making it accessible and affordable for Malaysian citizens. Expats are also eligible for public healthcare services, although they may pay slightly higher fees.

- **Private Healthcare:** Private healthcare facilities offer a higher standard of care, with shorter waiting times, more modern equipment, and a wider range of specialists. However, private healthcare can be significantly more expensive than public healthcare.

Health Insurance: Essential for Peace of Mind

It's highly advisable for retirees to have comprehensive health insurance that covers the costs of private healthcare services, medical emergencies, and evacuations. The cost of health insurance will vary depending on your age, health condition, and the level of coverage you choose.

Staying Active and Social: Maintaining a Fulfilling Lifestyle

Maintaining an active and social lifestyle is important for both physical and mental well-being during retirement.

- **Exercise Regularly:** Find activities you enjoy, such as walking, swimming, cycling, or joining a gym, to stay active and maintain your fitness.

- **Join Social Clubs and Activities:** Connect with like-minded people by joining social clubs, hobby groups, or expat organizations.

- **Volunteer:** Giving back to the community through volunteering can provide a sense of purpose and fulfillment.

- **Stay Connected with Family and Friends:** Maintain regular contact with your family and friends back home, either through phone calls, video chats, or visits.

Embracing Retirement in Malaysia: A New Chapter of Life

Retiring in Malaysia offers the chance to embrace a new chapter of life, filled with new experiences, cultural discoveries, and a more relaxed and fulfilling lifestyle. By understanding the benefits, the practical considerations, and the lifestyle you can expect, you can make informed decisions and create a retirement plan that aligns with your dreams and aspirations.

With its affordability, warm climate, diverse culture, friendly people, and abundance of opportunities for exploration and personal growth, Malaysia can be a truly rewarding place to spend your golden years.

CHAPTER TWENTY-FOUR: Investing in Malaysia: Opportunities and Considerations

Beyond its appeal as a place to live, work, and retire, Malaysia also presents attractive opportunities for investment, thanks to its robust economy, strategic location, and government initiatives aimed at attracting foreign capital. This chapter will explore the various investment avenues available in Malaysia, delving into the potential benefits, the risks involved, and the key considerations for making informed investment decisions.

Why Invest in Malaysia: A Compelling Case

Malaysia has consistently attracted foreign direct investment (FDI), consistently ranking among the top recipients of FDI in Southeast Asia. Several factors contribute to Malaysia's attractiveness as an investment destination:

Strategic Location: A Gateway to Southeast Asia

Malaysia occupies a strategic position in the heart of Southeast Asia, providing easy access to a vast regional market of over 650 million people. Its well-developed infrastructure, including ports, airports, and highways, facilitates trade and connectivity with neighboring countries.

Stable Political Environment: A Foundation for Confidence

Malaysia boasts a stable political environment, with a long history of peaceful transitions of power and a government committed to economic growth and development. This stability provides investors with confidence and predictability, reducing political risks.

Robust Economy: Growth and Diversification

Malaysia's economy has consistently grown over the past few decades, transitioning from a reliance on agriculture and natural resources to a more diversified and knowledge-based economy. The country has established itself as a hub for manufacturing, technology, finance, tourism, and healthcare, offering diverse opportunities for investment.

Business-Friendly Policies: Attracting Foreign Capital

The Malaysian government has implemented business-friendly policies aimed at attracting foreign investment, including tax incentives, streamlined business registration processes, and investment promotion agencies that provide support and guidance to foreign investors.

Skilled Workforce: Human Capital Advantage

Malaysia has a relatively young and educated workforce, with a growing pool of skilled professionals and technicians. The government has invested heavily in education and training, ensuring a steady supply of talent to meet the needs of various industries.

Cost Competitiveness: Lower Operating Expenses

Compared to many developed countries, Malaysia offers a cost-competitive environment for businesses, with lower labor costs, operating expenses, and property prices. This cost advantage can translate into higher profitability for investors.

Investment Opportunities: A Diverse Range of Options

Malaysia offers a diverse range of investment opportunities across various sectors:

Stock Market: Investing in Publicly Listed Companies

The Bursa Malaysia, the country's stock exchange, provides a platform for investors to participate in the growth of publicly listed companies. You can invest in stocks, bonds, and other securities, potentially earning capital gains and dividends.

Real Estate: Capital Appreciation and Rental Income

The Malaysian real estate market offers opportunities for capital appreciation and rental income. Foreigners are generally allowed to purchase certain types of properties, subject to minimum purchase price requirements.

Bonds: Fixed Income and Government Securities

Investing in bonds, particularly government bonds, offers a relatively safe and stable investment option, providing fixed income and a lower risk profile compared to stocks.

Unit Trusts and Mutual Funds: Diversified Investments

Unit trusts and mutual funds pool money from multiple investors to invest in a diversified portfolio of assets, such as stocks, bonds, and property. This diversification helps spread risk and potentially enhance returns.

Private Equity: Investing in Private Companies

Private equity investments involve providing capital to private companies, typically those with high growth potential. These investments can offer higher returns, but they also carry higher risks.

Venture Capital: Supporting Startups and Innovation

Venture capital investments support early-stage companies with high growth potential, particularly those in technology, innovation, and emerging industries. These investments can generate significant returns, but they are also associated with high risks.

Islamic Finance: Ethical and Sharia-Compliant Investments

Malaysia is a global leader in Islamic finance, offering a range of investment products and services that comply with Sharia principles. Islamic finance prohibits investments in industries considered unethical or harmful, such as alcohol, gambling, and pork products.

Investment Risks: Navigating the Uncertainties

All investments carry inherent risks, and Malaysia is no exception. Understanding the potential risks can help you make more informed investment decisions and mitigate potential losses.

Economic Risks: Fluctuations and Downturns

Economic fluctuations, global downturns, or changes in government policies can impact investment returns. Malaysia's economy is export-oriented and can be affected by global demand, commodity prices, and currency fluctuations.

Political Risks: Policy Changes and Instability

While Malaysia has a relatively stable political environment, policy changes, political instability, or regulatory changes can affect investment sentiment and potentially impact returns.

Market Risks: Volatility and Fluctuations

The stock market and real estate market can be volatile, with prices fluctuating based on market sentiment, economic conditions, and other factors. Investments in these markets can experience losses if prices decline.

Currency Risks: Exchange Rate Fluctuations

Currency fluctuations can impact the value of investments, particularly for foreign investors. If the Malaysian Ringgit weakens against your home currency, your investments may be worth less when converted back to your home currency.

Fraud and Scams: Protecting Yourself from Unscrupulous Schemes

Investment scams and fraudulent schemes can target unsuspecting investors. Be cautious of investment offers that promise unrealistically high returns or require you to invest large sums of money upfront. Always verify the legitimacy of investment companies and seek professional advice before making any investment decisions.

Investment Considerations: Key Factors to Assess

Before making any investment decisions in Malaysia, it's essential to conduct thorough research, assess the potential risks and rewards, and seek professional advice to align your investments with your financial goals and risk tolerance.

1. Investment Objectives: What Are Your Goals?

Clearly define your investment objectives, whether you're seeking capital appreciation, regular income, long-term growth, or a combination of these. Your investment goals will guide your investment choices and the level of risk you're willing to take.

2. Risk Tolerance: How Much Risk Can You Handle?

Assess your risk tolerance, which is the level of potential losses you're comfortable with. Investments carry varying degrees of risk, and it's crucial to choose investments that align with your risk appetite.

3. Time Horizon: How Long Will You Invest?

Your investment time horizon, or the length of time you plan to hold your investments, will influence your investment choices. Long-term investments, such as those held for retirement, can tolerate more risk than short-term investments.

4. Investment Expertise: Do You Need Professional Guidance?

Consider your level of investment expertise. If you're unfamiliar with the Malaysian investment landscape or specific investment products, seek professional advice from financial advisors, investment consultants, or wealth managers.

5. Due Diligence: Research and Verification

Conduct thorough due diligence on any investment opportunities, researching the company, the industry, the market conditions, and the associated risks. Verify the legitimacy of investment companies and seek independent advice before making any decisions.

6. Legal and Regulatory Framework: Understanding the Rules

Familiarize yourself with the legal and regulatory framework governing investments in Malaysia. Ensure you comply with all regulations, including those related to foreign ownership, tax liabilities, and reporting requirements.

7. Tax Implications: Minimizing Your Liabilities

Understand the tax implications of your investments. Malaysia has a territorial tax system, meaning that you are generally only taxed on income earned within the country. However, there may be tax exemptions or deductions available for certain types of investments.

8. Exit Strategy: Planning for the Future

Develop an exit strategy for your investments, considering how and when you plan to sell or liquidate your assets. Factor in potential market conditions, tax implications, and your overall financial goals.

Seeking Professional Advice: Guidance for Informed Decisions

Navigating the investment landscape in a foreign country can be complex. Seeking professional advice from qualified financial advisors, investment consultants, or wealth managers can provide valuable guidance, helping you:

- **Assess Your Financial Goals and Risk Tolerance:** A financial advisor can help you define your investment objectives, assess your risk tolerance, and develop an investment strategy tailored to your needs.

- **Identify Suitable Investment Opportunities:** Based on your financial goals and risk profile, a financial advisor can recommend suitable investment options, such as stocks, bonds, property, or unit trusts.

- **Manage Your Investment Portfolio:** A financial advisor can help you manage your investment portfolio, monitoring its performance, rebalancing assets as needed, and making adjustments based on market conditions.

- **Optimize Tax Liabilities:** A financial advisor can help you understand the tax implications of your investments and recommend strategies to minimize your tax liabilities.

Embracing Investment Opportunities: Growing Your Wealth in Malaysia

Malaysia's robust economy, strategic location, and business-friendly policies create a favorable environment for investment.

By carefully considering your investment objectives, risk tolerance, and time horizon, conducting thorough due diligence, and seeking professional advice, you can embrace the investment opportunities that Malaysia offers, potentially growing your wealth and achieving your financial goals. Remember, every investment carries inherent risks, and diversification is key to mitigating potential losses and achieving long-term financial success.

CHAPTER TWENTY-FIVE: Adapting to Life in Malaysia: Tips for a Smooth Transition

You've done your research, secured your visa, found a place to live, and maybe even landed a job. You're officially an expat in Malaysia! Excitement mingles with a touch of apprehension as you step into this new chapter of your life. Adapting to a new country, even one as welcoming as Malaysia, takes time and effort. But with the right mindset, a dose of cultural sensitivity, and a willingness to embrace new experiences, you can navigate the transition smoothly and create a fulfilling and enriching life in your new Malaysian home. This chapter will equip you with valuable tips and insights to help you adjust to the Malaysian way of life, overcome potential challenges, and embrace the opportunities that this diverse and dynamic nation has to offer.

Embracing the Cultural Shift: A Mindset for Adaptation

Moving to a new country involves more than just a change of scenery; it's a cultural shift that requires a flexible mindset and a willingness to adapt to new customs, values, and ways of life.

1. Open Your Mind: Embrace Curiosity and Flexibility

Approach your new Malaysian experience with an open mind and a genuine curiosity to learn and understand a different culture. Be prepared to encounter customs, beliefs, and values that may differ from your own. Embrace the opportunity to expand your horizons, challenge your assumptions, and see the world from a different perspective.

Flexibility is key to adapting smoothly. Be willing to adjust your expectations, try new things, and go with the flow. Things may not always work the same way as they did in your home country, and that's okay. Embrace the differences, learn from them, and allow yourself to be surprised by the unique aspects of Malaysian culture.

2. Embrace the Learning Curve: Patience and a Sense of Humor

Adapting to a new culture is a learning process, and it's natural to make mistakes or encounter misunderstandings along the way. Be patient with yourself, allow yourself time to adjust, and don't be afraid to ask questions. Most Malaysians are happy to share their culture and help you navigate the nuances.

A sense of humor can go a long way in easing the transition. Laugh at yourself when you make mistakes, embrace the unexpected, and appreciate the humorous side of cultural differences. A lighthearted approach can help you maintain a positive outlook and navigate challenges with grace.

3. Challenge Stereotypes: Seek Authentic Experiences

Avoid making generalizations or assumptions based on stereotypes or preconceived notions. Every culture has its unique complexities, and Malaysia is no exception. Seek authentic experiences, engage with locals, ask questions, and challenge your own biases to gain a deeper understanding of the Malaysian people and their way of life.

4. Find Common Ground: Connecting Beyond Differences

While cultural differences are inevitable, remember that people from all cultures share common values and aspirations. Focus on finding common ground, building relationships based on mutual respect, empathy, and shared interests.

5. Celebrate Diversity: Embrace the Cultural Mosaic

Malaysia's multicultural society is a vibrant tapestry woven from the traditions, values, and customs of its diverse ethnic groups. Embrace the opportunity to learn about different cultures, participate in festivals, try new cuisines, and experience the richness of this cultural mosaic. Celebrating diversity can broaden your horizons, enrich your life, and make your Malaysian experience more rewarding.

Building a Support System: Connecting with Others

Moving to a new country can be a lonely experience, particularly during the initial stages of settling in. Building a support system of friends, colleagues, and mentors can provide a sense of belonging, ease the transition, and offer valuable guidance as you navigate your new life in Malaysia.

1. Reach Out to Expat Communities: Finding Familiar Ground

Connecting with other expats can provide a sense of familiarity and support, especially during the early days when you're still finding your feet. Expat communities offer a shared understanding of the challenges and joys of living abroad, and they often organize social events, activities, and support groups that can help you feel more connected.

- **Online Forums and Social Media Groups:** Online platforms like InterNations, Expat.com, and Facebook groups dedicated to expats in Malaysia are great resources for connecting with others, asking questions, sharing experiences, and finding out about social events.

- **Expat Organizations and Clubs:** Many expat organizations and clubs cater to specific nationalities or interests, offering a chance to meet like-minded individuals and engage in social activities.

- **International Schools and Churches:** If you have children attending international schools or are involved in a church community, these can be great places to connect with other expat families.

2. Connect with Locals: Building Bridges of Friendship

While connecting with other expats can provide initial support, building friendships with Malaysians can enrich your experience and provide a deeper understanding of the local culture. Be proactive in initiating conversations, expressing interest in their culture, and accepting invitations to social gatherings.

- **Language Exchange:** Participating in a language exchange is a great way to practice your Bahasa Malaysia, learn about Malaysian culture, and connect with locals.

- **Hobby Groups and Activities:** Joining clubs, sports teams, or other groups related to your interests can help you meet Malaysians who share your passions.

- **Volunteering:** Volunteering for a local charity or organization is a rewarding way to give back to the community and connect with Malaysians who are passionate about similar causes.

3. Networking: Building Professional Connections

If you're working in Malaysia, your workplace can be a valuable source of social connections. Take the initiative to get to know your colleagues, participate in company events, and accept invitations to after-work gatherings.

Networking events, organized by industry associations or other professional groups, offer opportunities to connect with people in your field, expand your professional circle, and gain valuable insights into the Malaysian business landscape.

4. Mentorship: Seeking Guidance and Support

Finding a mentor, whether it's a fellow expat who has been living in Malaysia for a while or a Malaysian colleague or friend, can provide invaluable guidance and support as you navigate your new life. A mentor can share their experiences, offer advice, introduce you to their network, and help you overcome challenges.

Overcoming Cultural Challenges: Navigating Differences with Sensitivity

Adapting to a new culture inevitably involves navigating cultural differences that can sometimes lead to misunderstandings or challenges. Being mindful of these nuances, approaching them with sensitivity, and seeking clarification when needed can help you build stronger relationships and avoid potential conflicts.

1. Communication Styles: Decoding Indirectness

Malaysian communication style tends to be more indirect and non-confrontational compared to some Western cultures. Directness and assertiveness, while common in some contexts, may be perceived as rude or aggressive in Malaysia.

Be mindful of your tone of voice, body language, and choice of words. Pay attention to nonverbal cues, as Malaysians often convey meaning through subtle gestures or facial expressions. If you're unsure about something, don't hesitate to ask for clarification.

2. Respect for Hierarchy: Acknowledging Authority

Malaysian culture places great importance on respect for elders and authority figures. When addressing someone older or of higher status, use appropriate honorific titles, such as "Encik" (Mr.), "Puan" (Mrs.), or "Cik" (Miss), before their name. Avoid being overly familiar or casual in your interactions, particularly in formal settings.

3. Religious Sensitivities: Respecting Diverse Beliefs

Malaysia is a multi-religious country, with Islam, Buddhism, Christianity, Hinduism, and other faiths coexisting harmoniously. Be respectful of religious sensitivities, dress modestly when visiting religious sites, and avoid making comments that could be interpreted as offensive or disrespectful.

During the month of Ramadan, when Muslims fast from dawn to dusk, it's respectful to refrain from eating or drinking in public during fasting hours.

4. Social Customs: Observing Etiquette

Malaysian social customs and etiquette may differ from your own. Here are some key customs to be aware of:

- **Removing Shoes:** It's customary to remove your shoes before entering a Malaysian home or a mosque.

- **Using Your Right Hand:** The right hand is considered clean in Malay culture and is used for eating, shaking hands, and giving or receiving items. Avoid using your left hand for these actions.

- **Avoiding Public Displays of Affection:** Public displays of affection, such as kissing or hugging, are generally frowned upon in Malaysia, particularly in conservative areas.

5. Patience and Understanding: Building Bridges of Empathy

Building cross-cultural relationships requires patience, understanding, and a willingness to embrace differences. Be prepared for things to move at a different pace, for communication styles to vary, and for social customs to be unique.

Embrace the learning process, ask questions, seek clarification, and be open to seeing the world from a different perspective. Building bridges of empathy and understanding is key to navigating cultural differences and creating meaningful connections.

Adapting to Daily Life: Finding Your Rhythm

Beyond the cultural adjustments, adapting to daily life in Malaysia involves navigating practical aspects, such as transportation, food, shopping, and healthcare.

1. Transportation: Getting Around with Ease

Malaysia offers a diverse range of transportation options, from efficient public transportation to ride-hailing services and private vehicles.

- **Public Transportation:** Major cities like Kuala Lumpur and Penang have extensive public transportation systems, including buses, trains, and light rail transit (LRT). Public transport is generally affordable and convenient, particularly for commuting within urban areas.

- **Ride-Hailing Services:** Ride-hailing services like Grab are widely available and offer a convenient and affordable alternative to taxis.

- **Driving:** If you prefer to drive, you can obtain a Malaysian driving license by converting your foreign license. However, traffic congestion can be a significant issue in major cities, particularly during peak hours.

2. Food: A Culinary Adventure

Malaysia is a food lover's paradise, offering a tantalizing array of cuisines and flavors. Embrace the opportunity to explore the diverse culinary landscape, from hawker centers and street food stalls to local restaurants and fine dining establishments.

- **Hawker Centers and Food Courts:** These bustling food havens offer a wide variety of dishes at affordable prices, making them a great option for experiencing local flavors.

- **Mamak Restaurants:** Run by Indian Muslims, Mamak restaurants are a unique Malaysian institution, serving a fusion of Indian, Malay, and Chinese dishes. They are often open 24 hours a day, making them a popular spot for late-night meals or casual hangouts.

- **Local Restaurants:** Explore different neighborhoods to discover hidden culinary gems and savor regional specialties.

- **Fine Dining:** Malaysia also offers a growing number of fine dining restaurants, showcasing innovative culinary creations and elevated dining experiences.

3. Shopping: From Malls to Markets

Malaysia is a shopper's delight, offering a diverse range of shopping experiences, from modern megamalls to bustling street markets and independent boutiques.

- **Malls:** Malaysian malls are air-conditioned havens that offer a dazzling array of shopping, dining, and entertainment options.

- **Street Markets:** For a more authentic and immersive experience, venture into the bustling street markets, where you can find everything from clothing and accessories to food, handicrafts, and electronics.

- **Independent Boutiques:** Explore heritage neighborhoods and online platforms to discover unique and locally made products from independent boutiques and craft shops.

4. Healthcare: Accessing Medical Services

Malaysia's healthcare system is generally well-regarded, offering both public and private options.

- **Public Healthcare:** The public healthcare system is heavily subsidized by the government, making it accessible and affordable for Malaysian citizens. Expats are also eligible for public healthcare services, although they may pay higher fees.

- **Private Healthcare:** Private healthcare facilities offer a higher standard of care, with shorter waiting times, more modern equipment, and a wider range of specialists. However, private healthcare can be significantly more expensive.

It's advisable for expats to have private health insurance to cover the costs of private healthcare services.

5. Language: Communicating Effectively

While English is widely spoken in Malaysia, learning some basic Bahasa Malaysia can enhance your daily interactions, facilitate communication, and show respect for the local culture.

- **Language Schools:** Enroll in a Bahasa Malaysia course at a language school.

- **Online Language Learning Platforms:** Utilize online language learning platforms, such as Duolingo or Babbel.

- **Language Exchange Partners:** Find a language exchange partner to practice speaking Bahasa Malaysia.

- **Immersion:** Surround yourself with the language by watching local TV shows, listening to Malaysian music, and engaging in conversations with Malaysians.

6. Social Etiquette: Navigating Customs with Grace

Understanding and adhering to local social etiquette is essential for building positive relationships and showing respect for Malaysian culture. Here are some key aspects of Malaysian social etiquette:

- **Greetings:** Use appropriate greetings, such as "Selamat pagi" (good morning), "Selamat tengah hari" (good afternoon), or "Selamat petang" (good evening), depending on the time of day.

- **Respect for Elders:** Address older people and authority figures with respect, using honorific titles.

- **Indirect Communication:** Malaysian communication style tends to be indirect and non-confrontational. Be mindful of your tone of voice and body language.

- **Body Language:** Avoid pointing with your index finger, showing the soles of your feet, or touching someone's head.

- **Dining Etiquette:** Use your right hand for eating, take small portions from shared dishes, and finish the food on your plate.

- **Gift-Giving:** Wrap gifts neatly and avoid giving alcohol or pork products to Muslims.

7. Safety and Security: Taking Sensible Precautions

Malaysia is generally a safe country, but it's always advisable to take precautions to protect your safety and belongings. Be aware of your surroundings, particularly in crowded areas, keep your valuables secure, and avoid walking alone at night in poorly lit or isolated areas.

8. Finding Your Community: Building Connections

Building a sense of community is essential for a fulfilling life in Malaysia. Connect with other expats, build friendships with locals, join social clubs or hobby groups, and participate in community events.

9. Embracing the Journey: Patience and a Positive Attitude

Adapting to a new country takes time and effort. Be patient with yourself, embrace the learning process, maintain a positive attitude, and celebrate the small victories along the way.

10. Seeking Support: Reaching Out When You Need It

Don't hesitate to reach out for support if you're feeling overwhelmed or facing challenges. Talk to friends, family, colleagues, or seek professional help from counselors or therapists if needed.

Thriving in Your New Home: Embracing the Malaysian Experience

Moving to Malaysia opens the door to a world of new experiences, cultural discoveries, and personal growth. By embracing the cultural shift, building a support system, navigating cultural differences with sensitivity, adapting to daily life, and maintaining a positive attitude, you can thrive in your new home and create a fulfilling and enriching life in this diverse and dynamic nation.

Printed in Great Britain
by Amazon